KATE HERBERT

WHAT CAN YOU SEE, ROSIE?

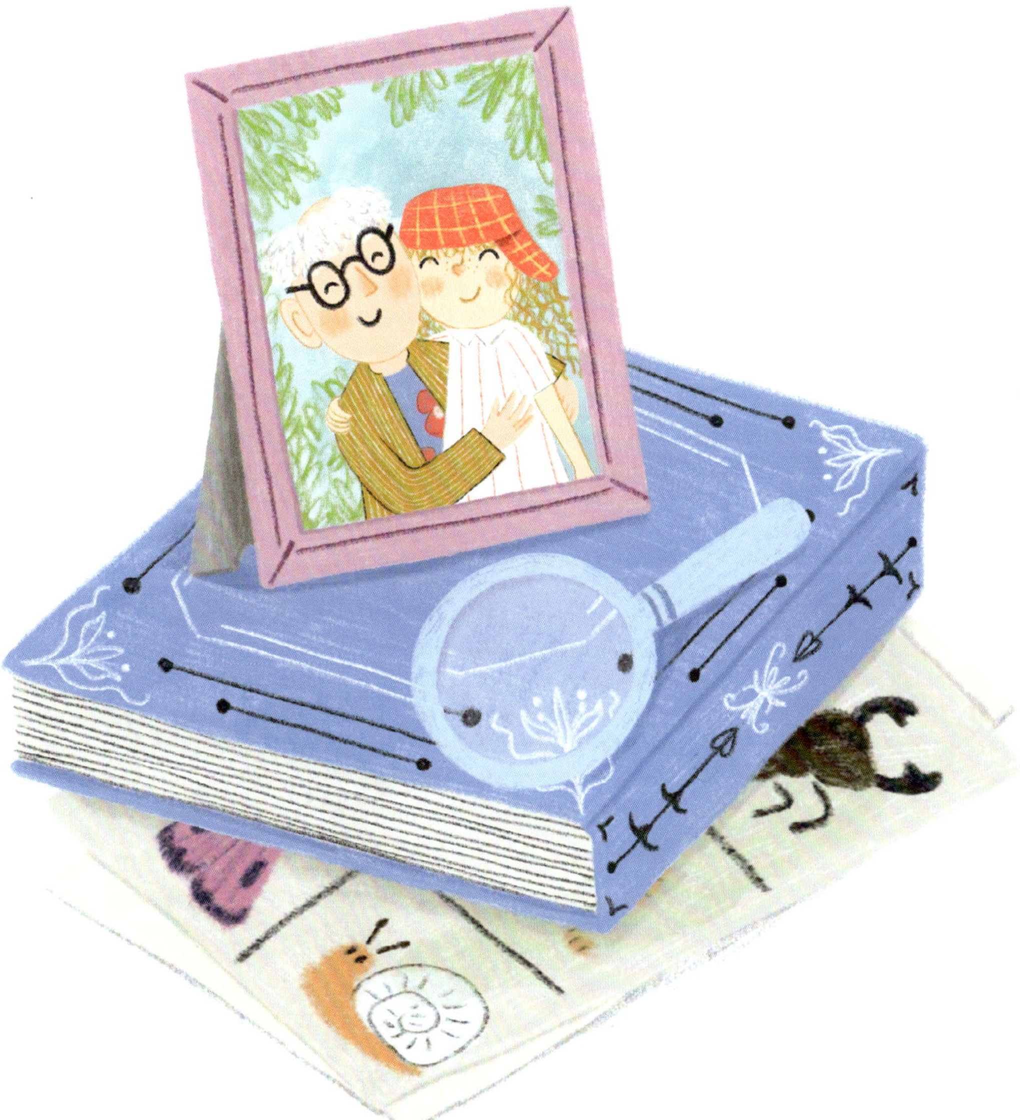

Collins

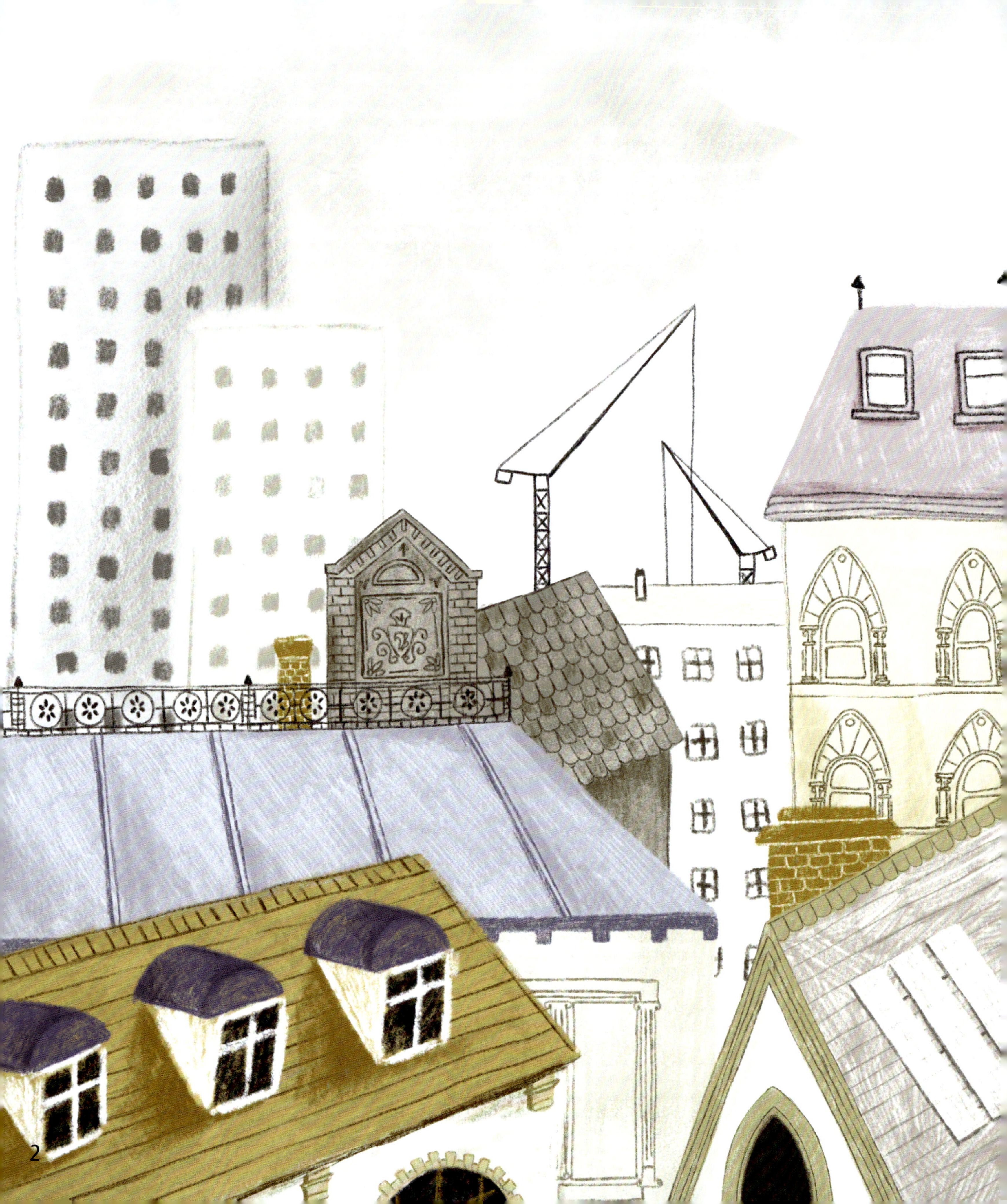

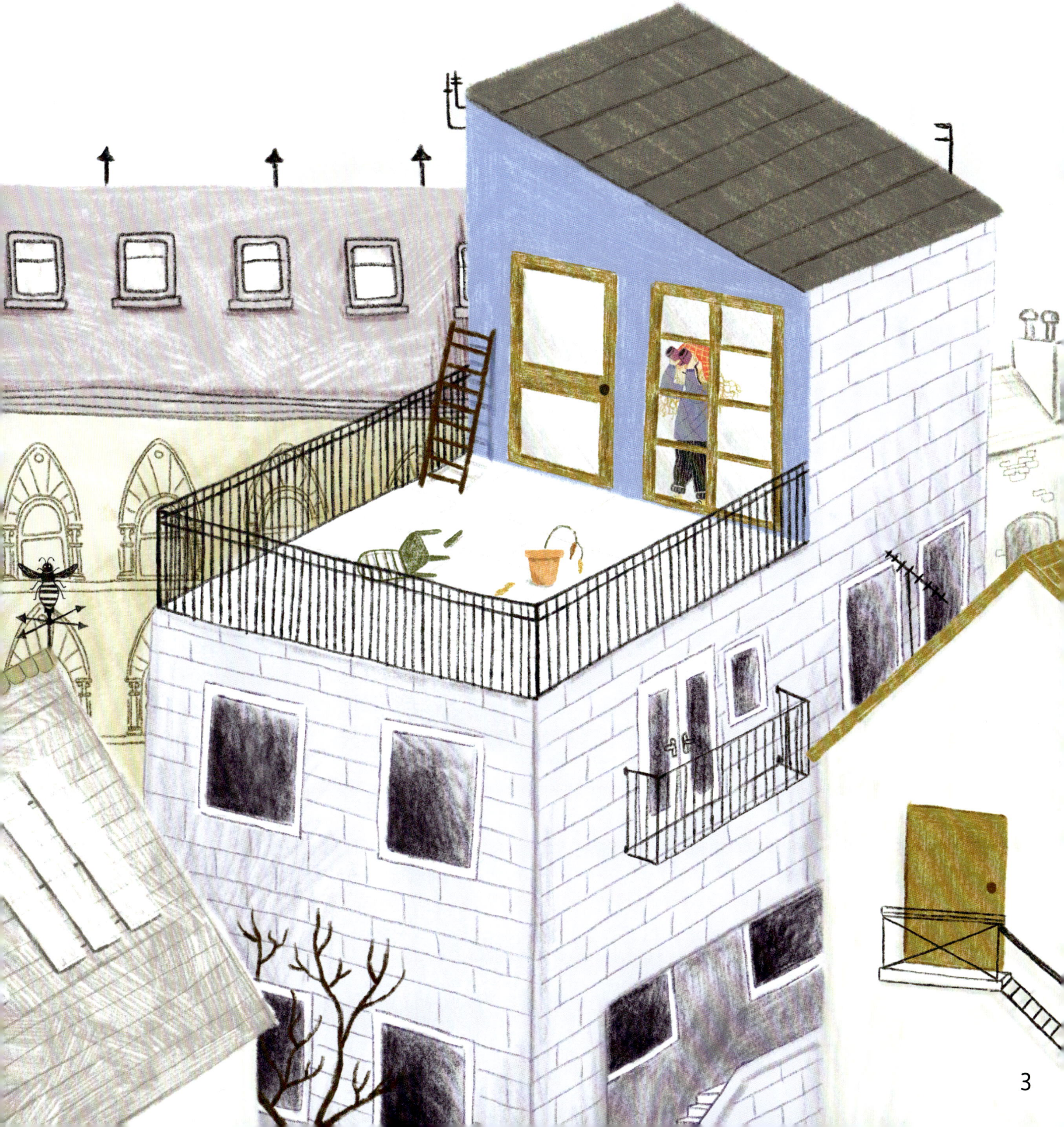

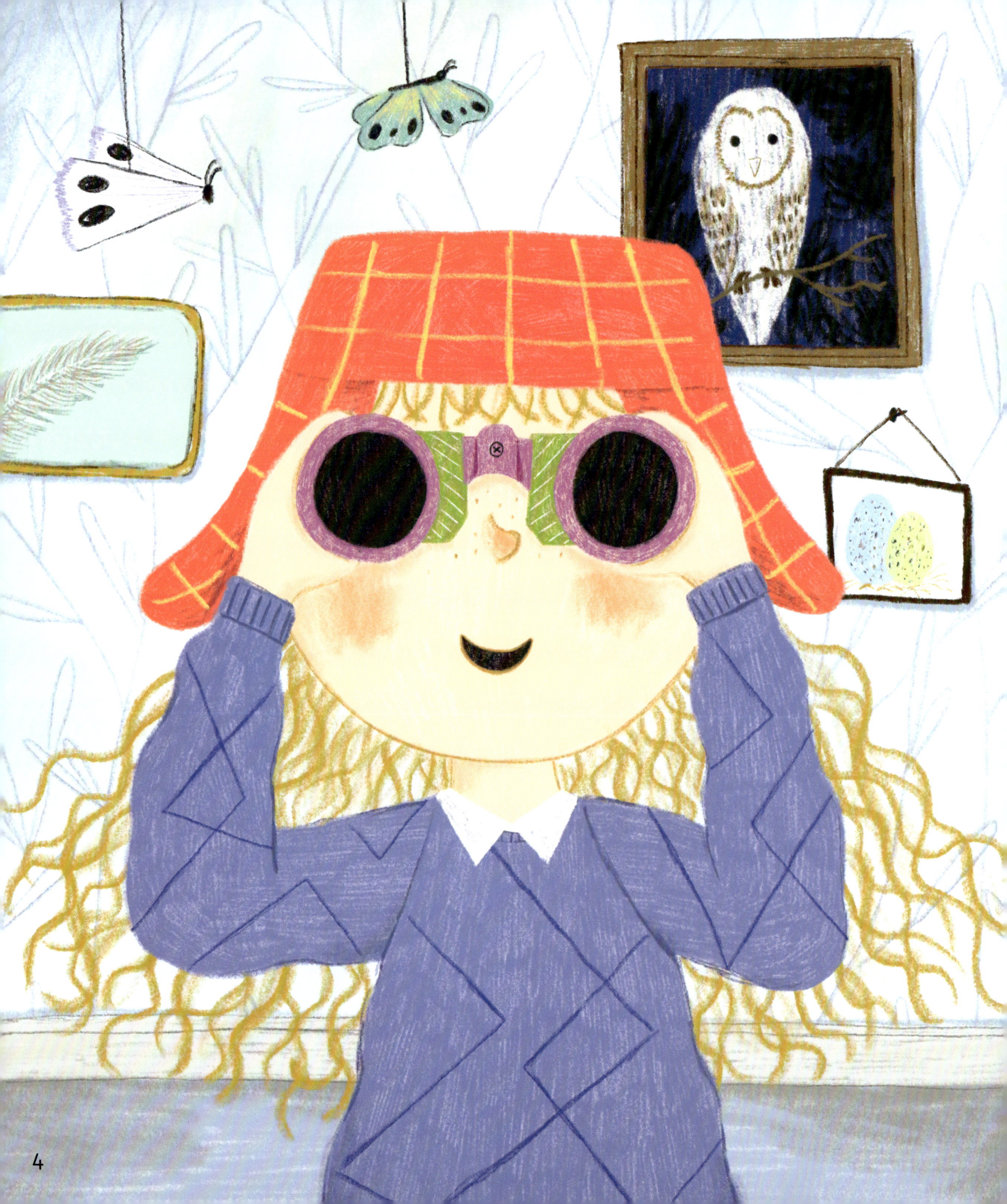

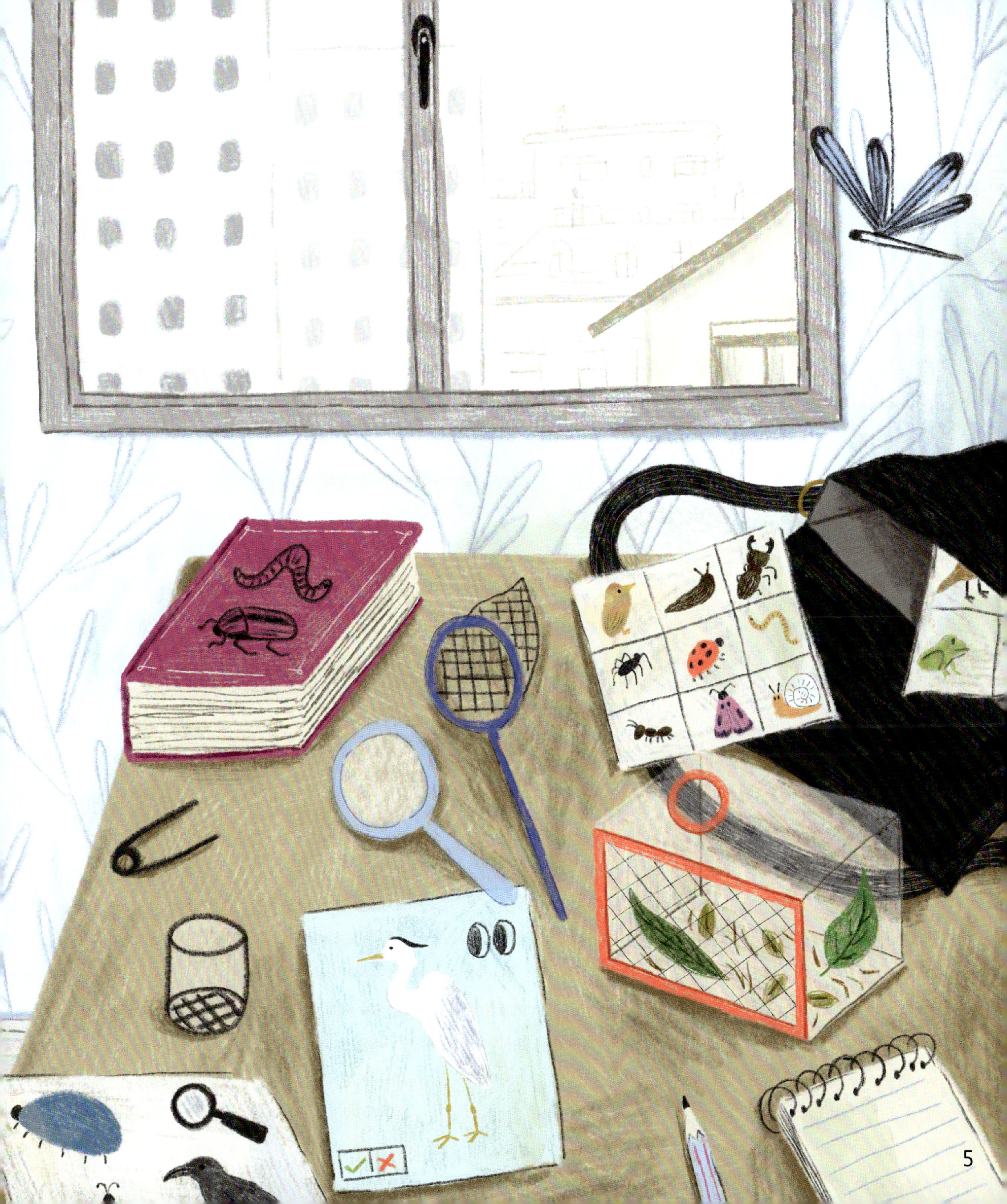

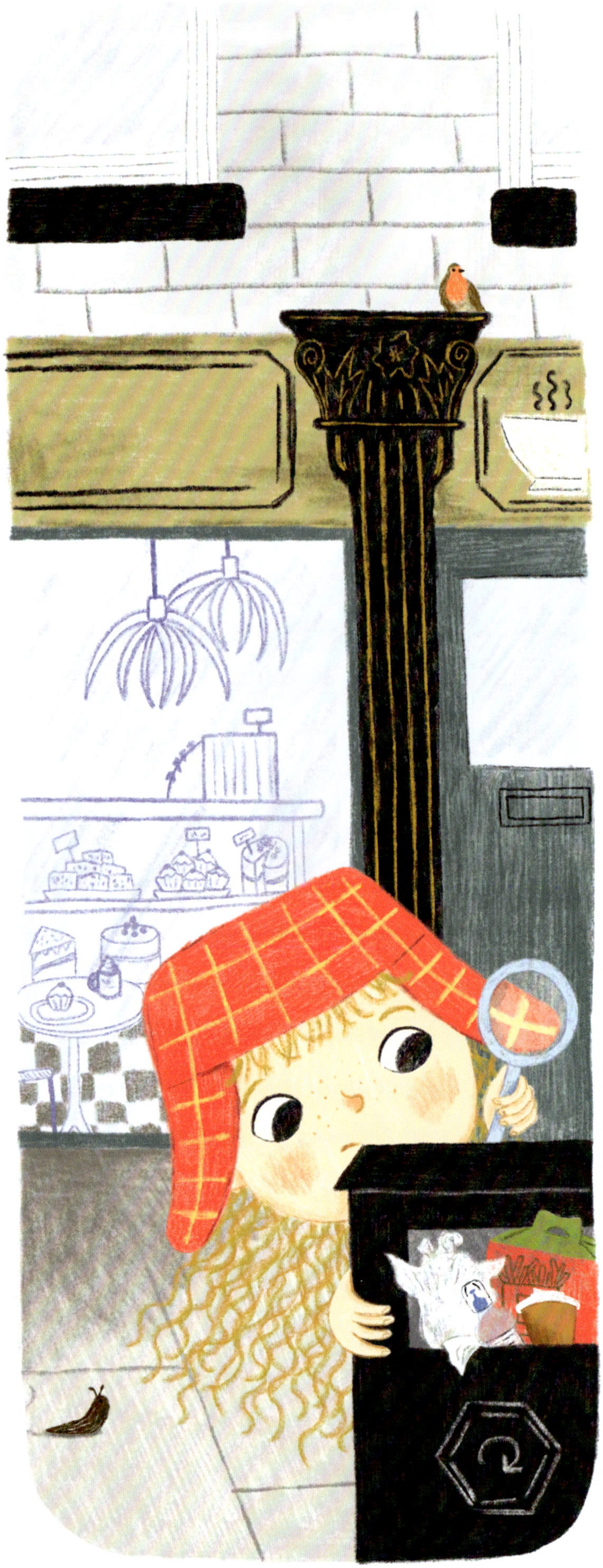

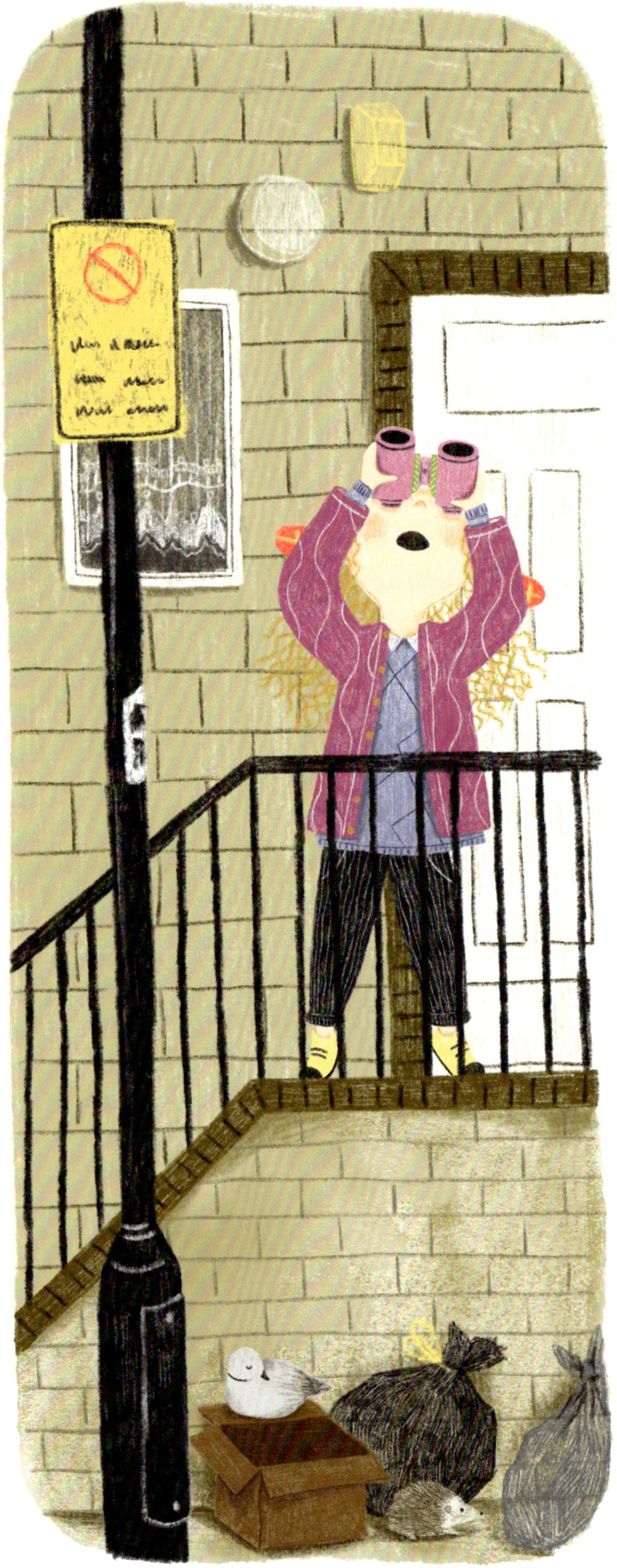

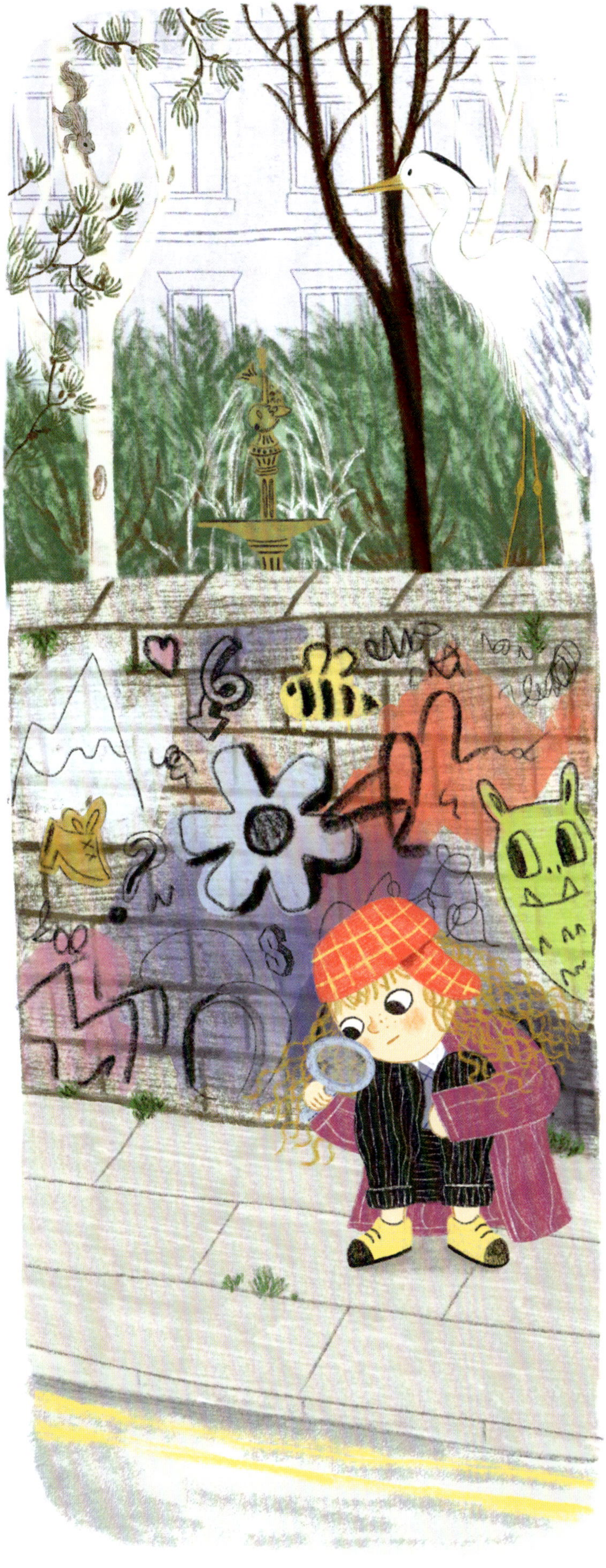
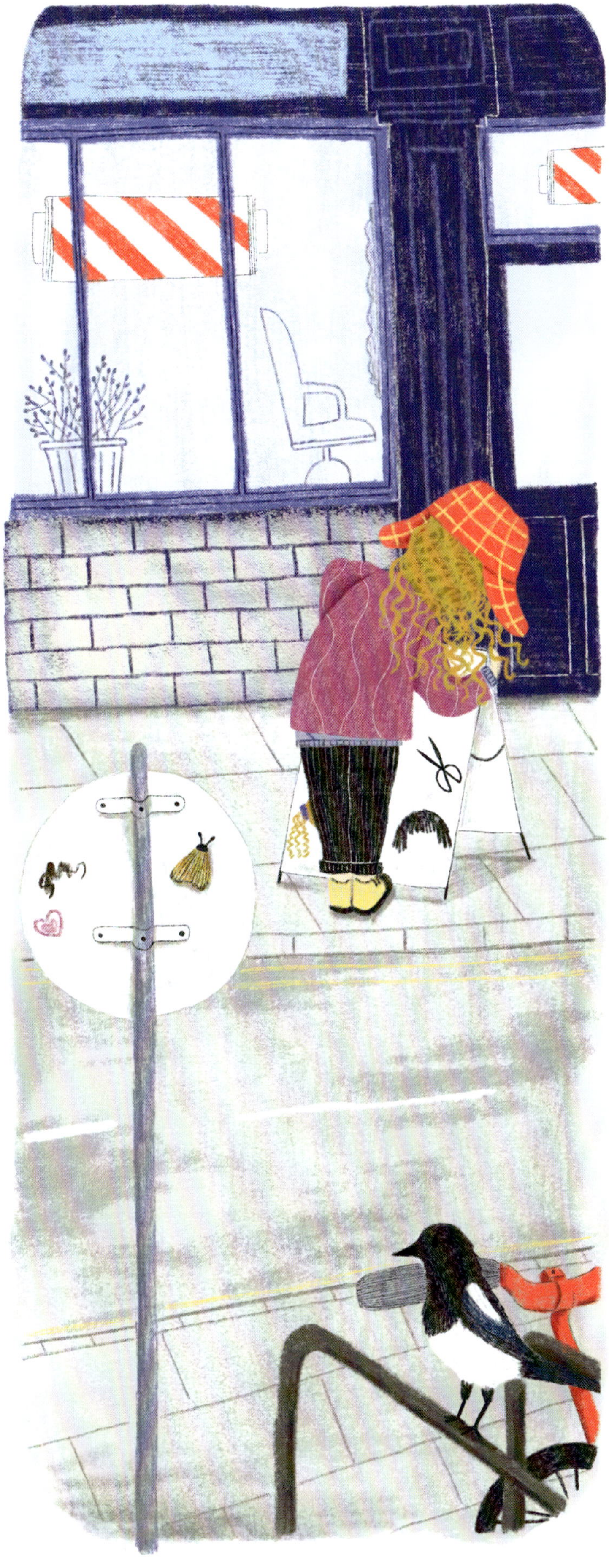

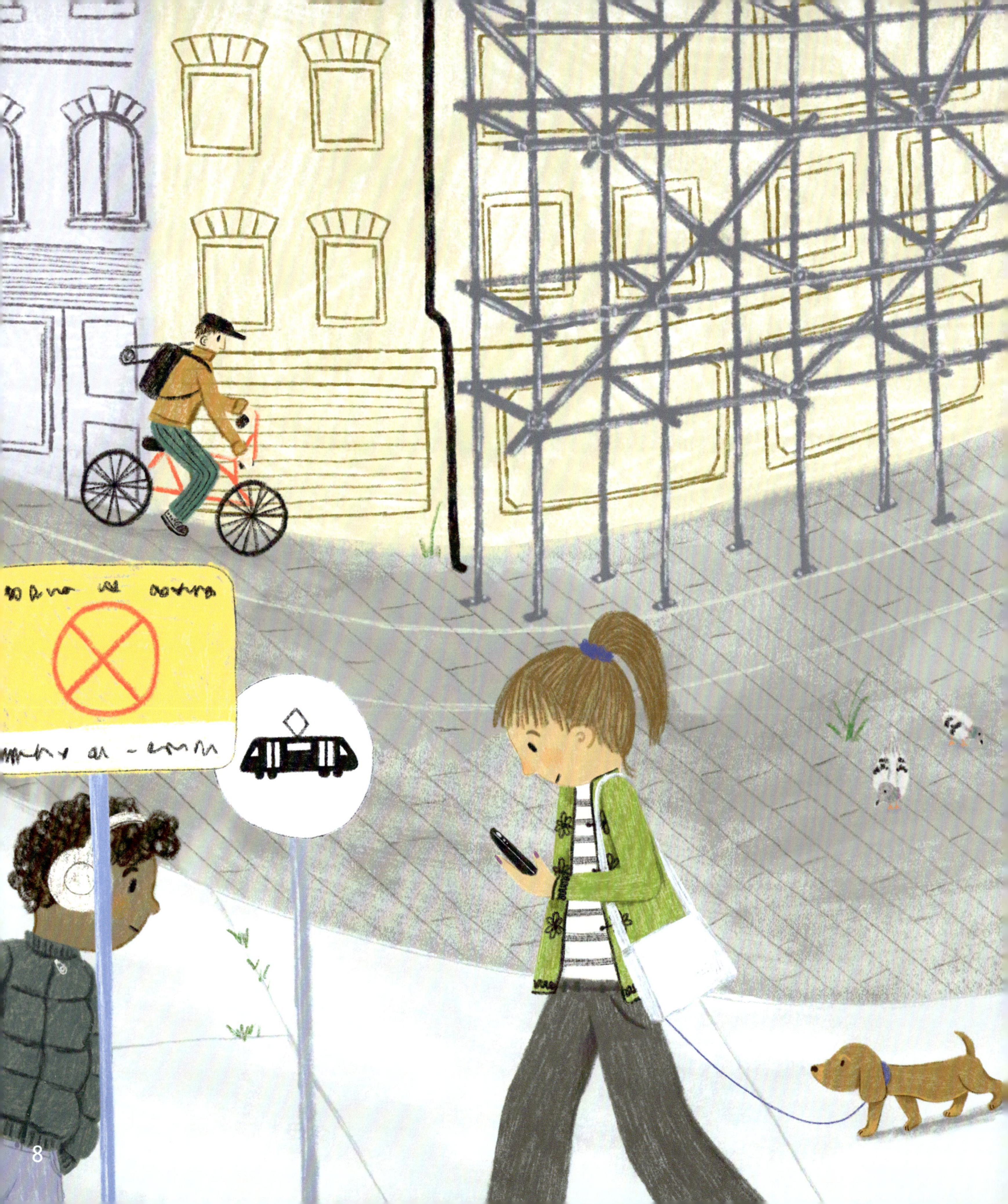

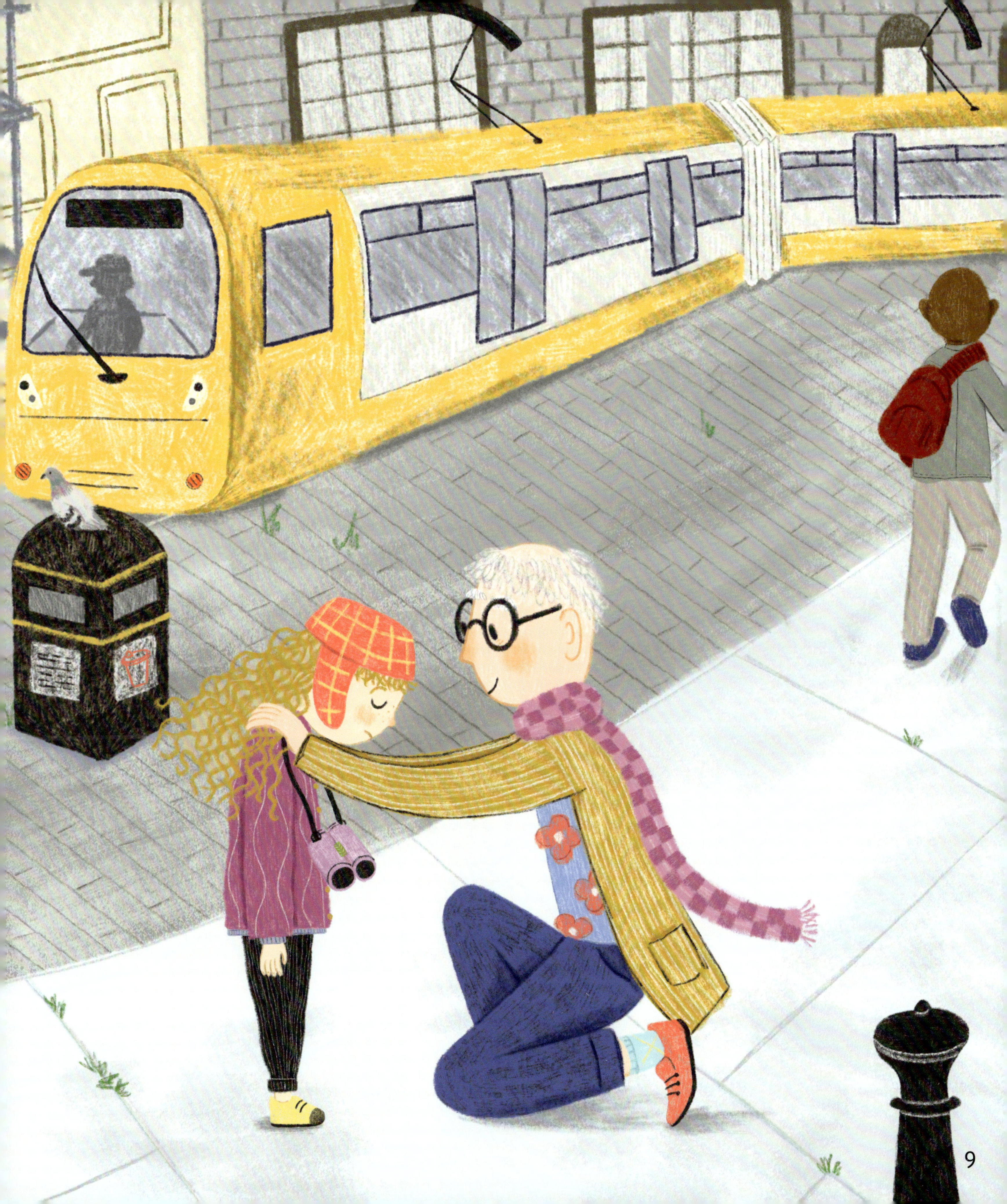

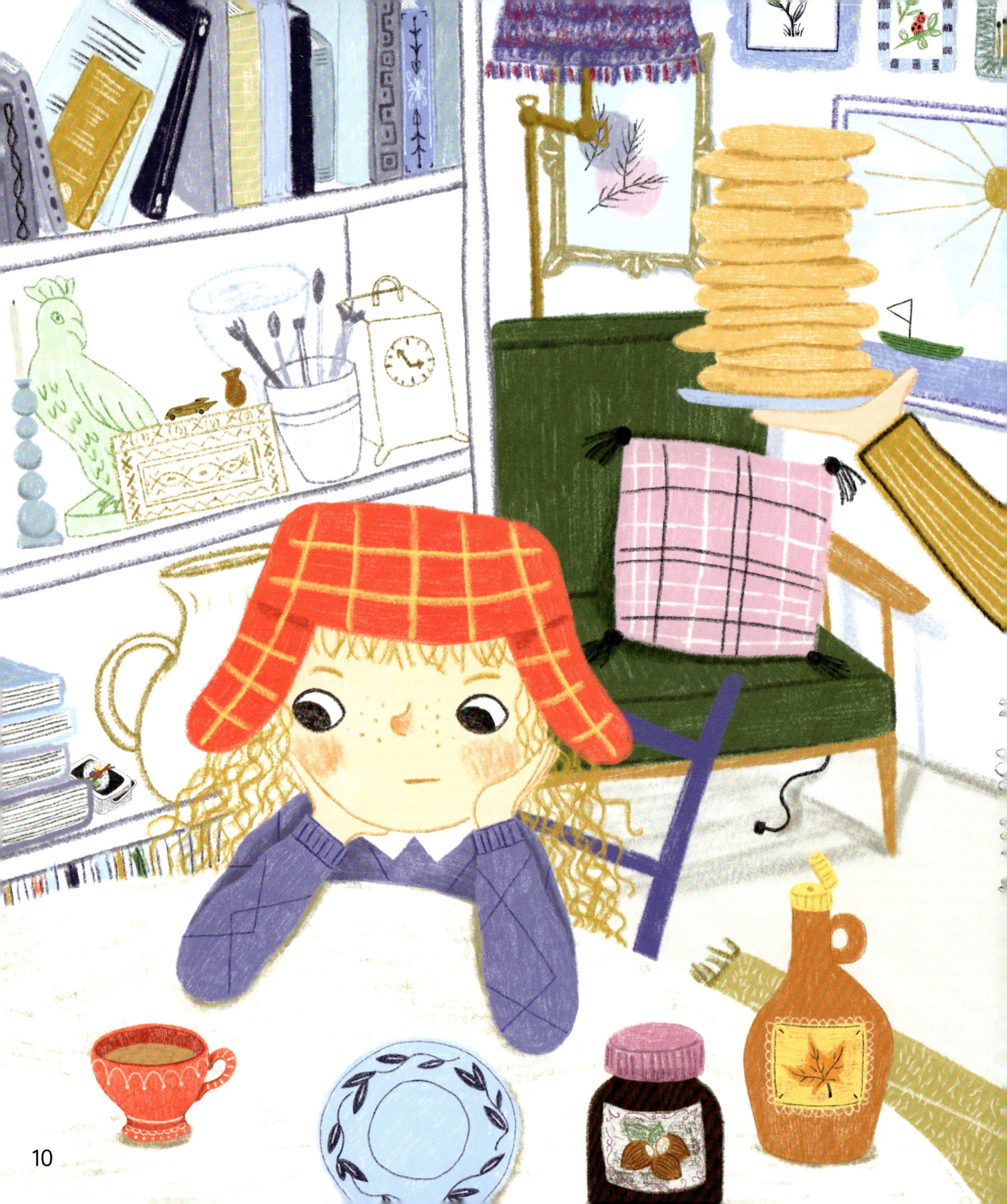

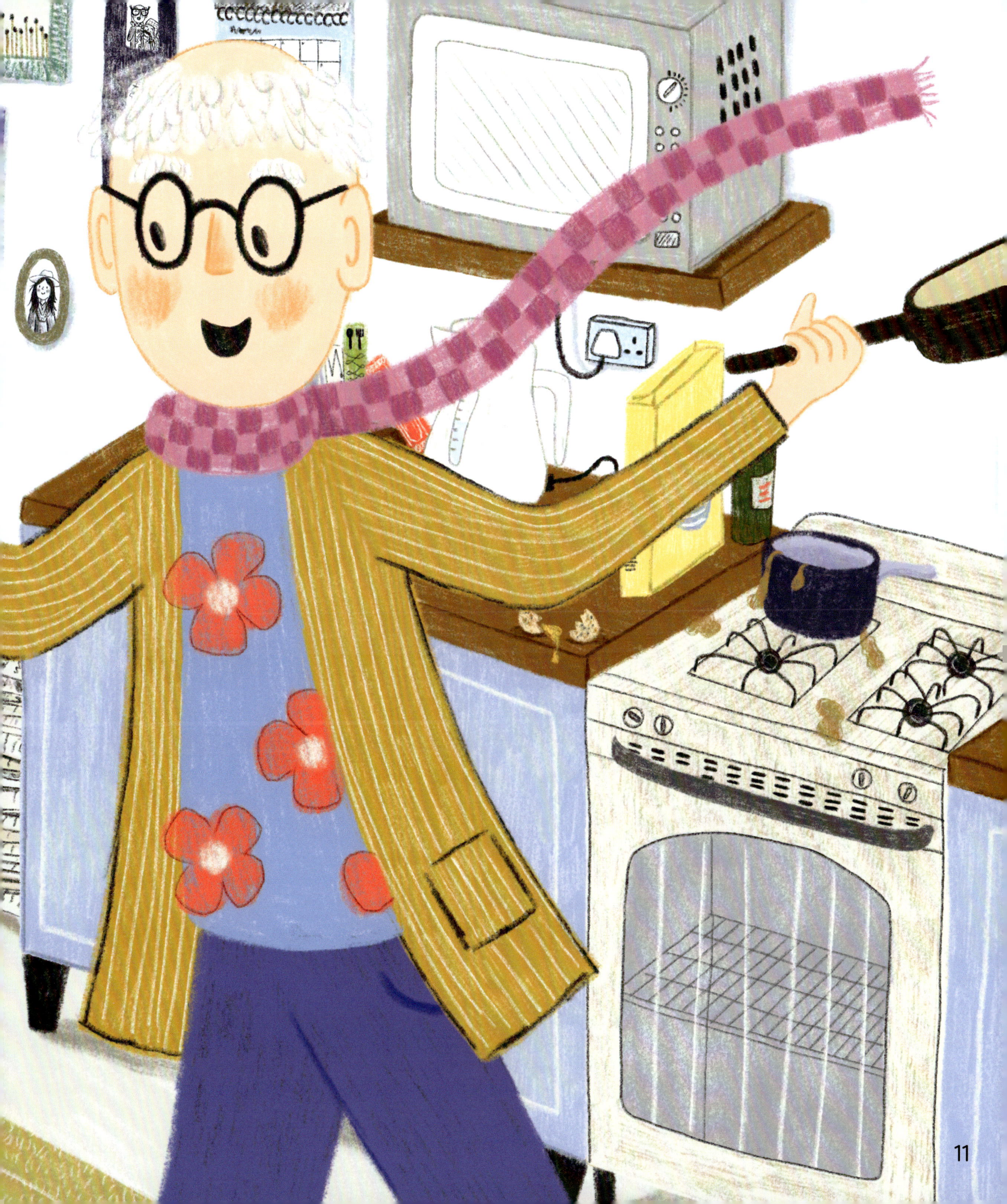

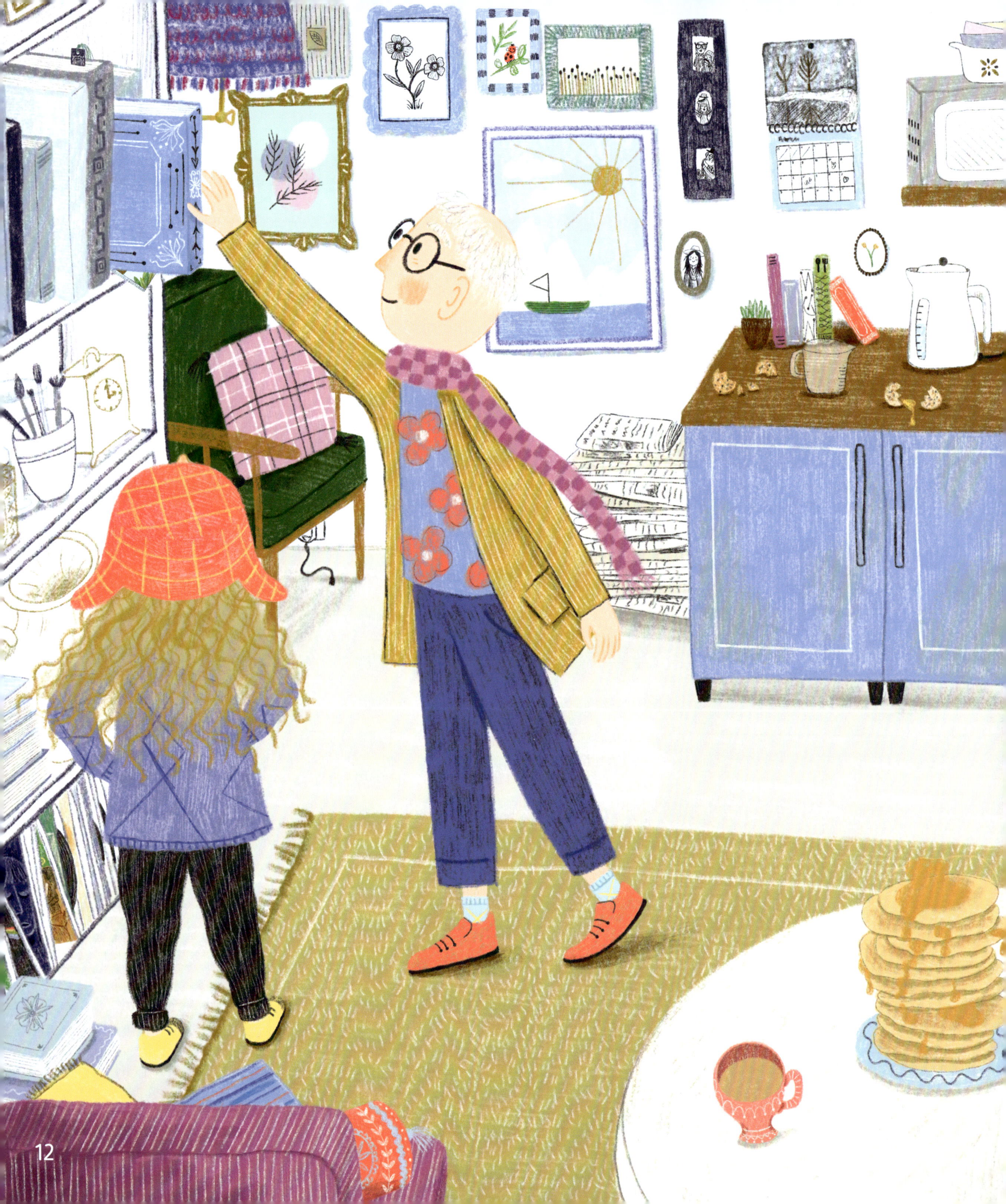

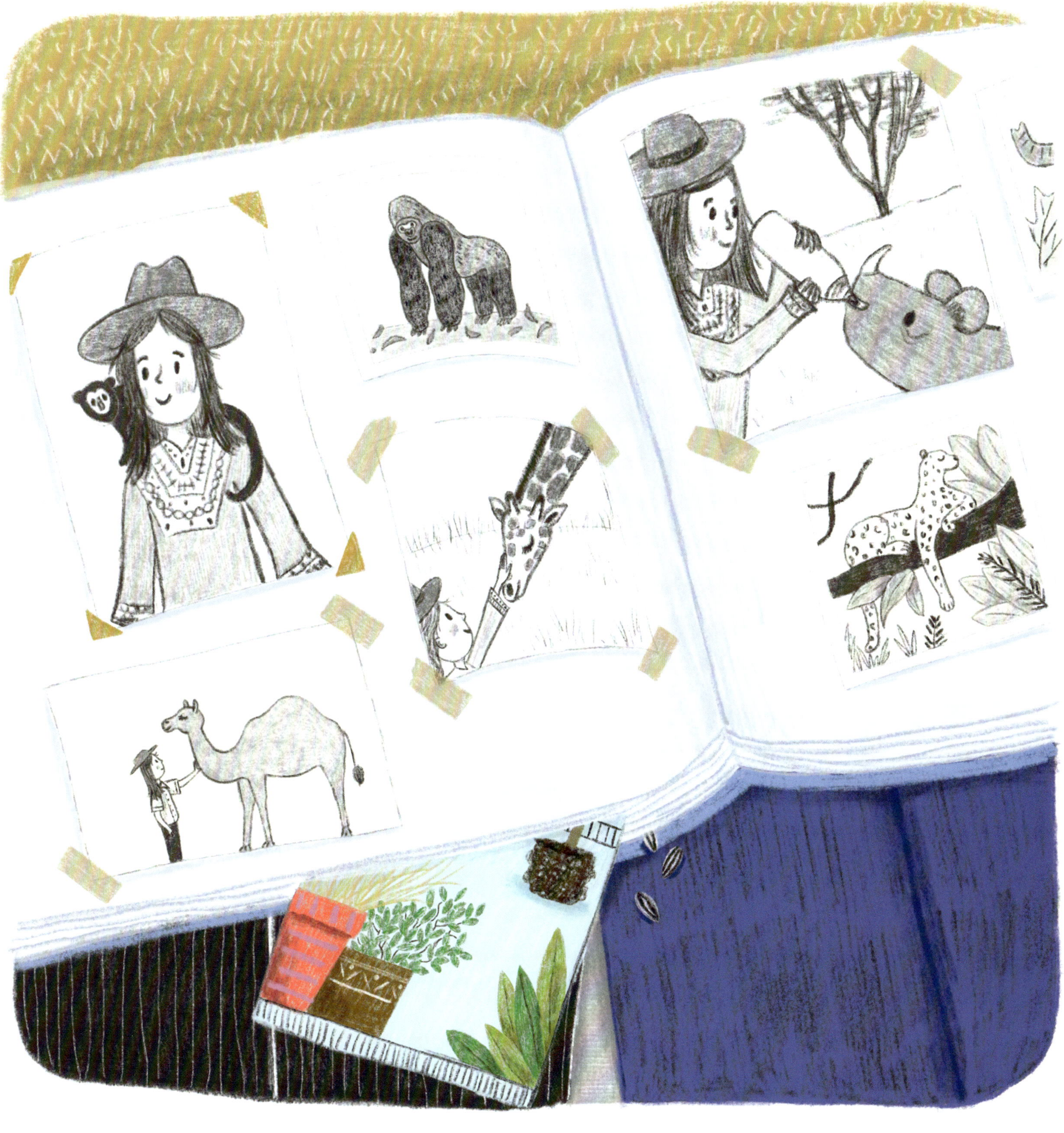

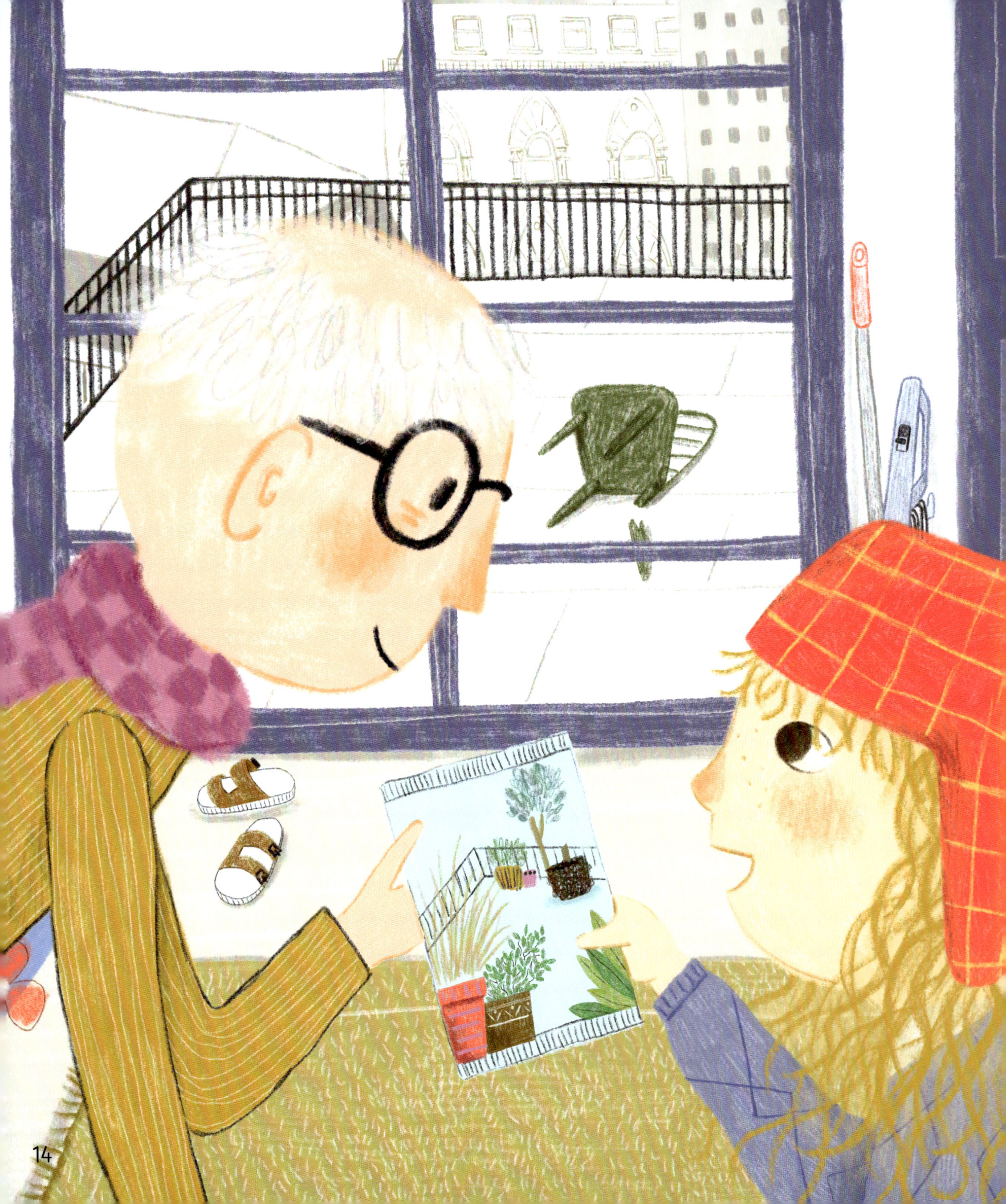

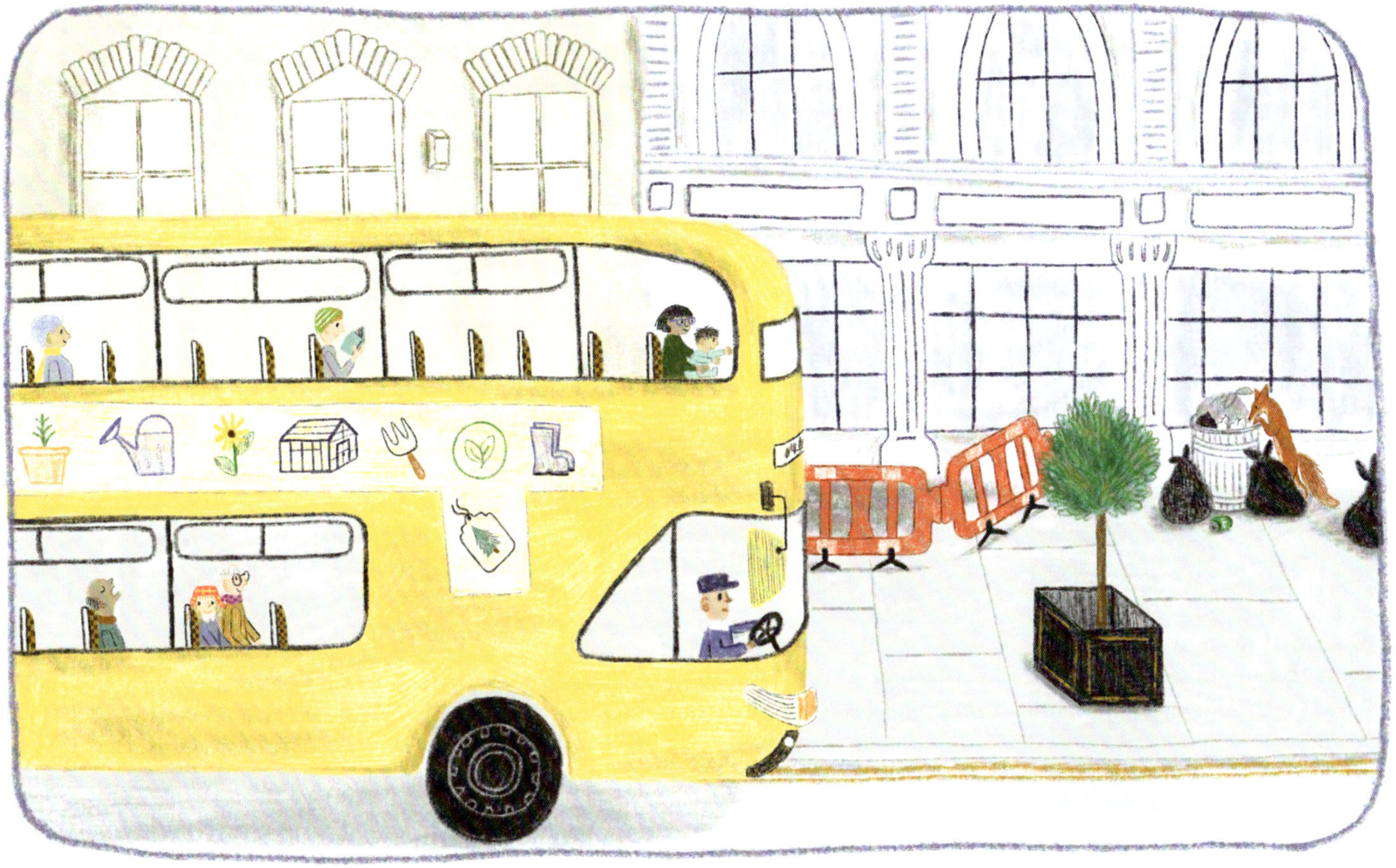

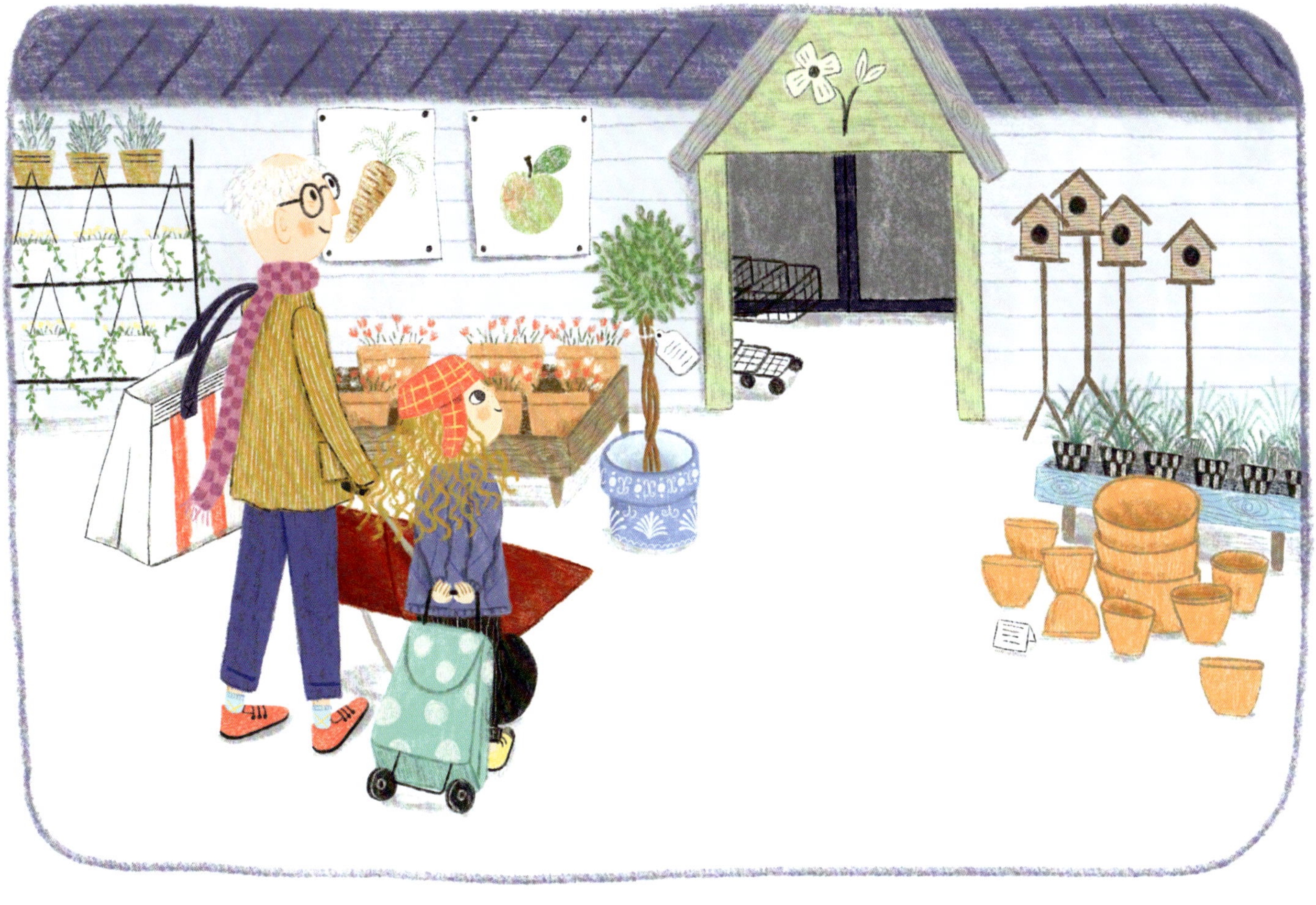

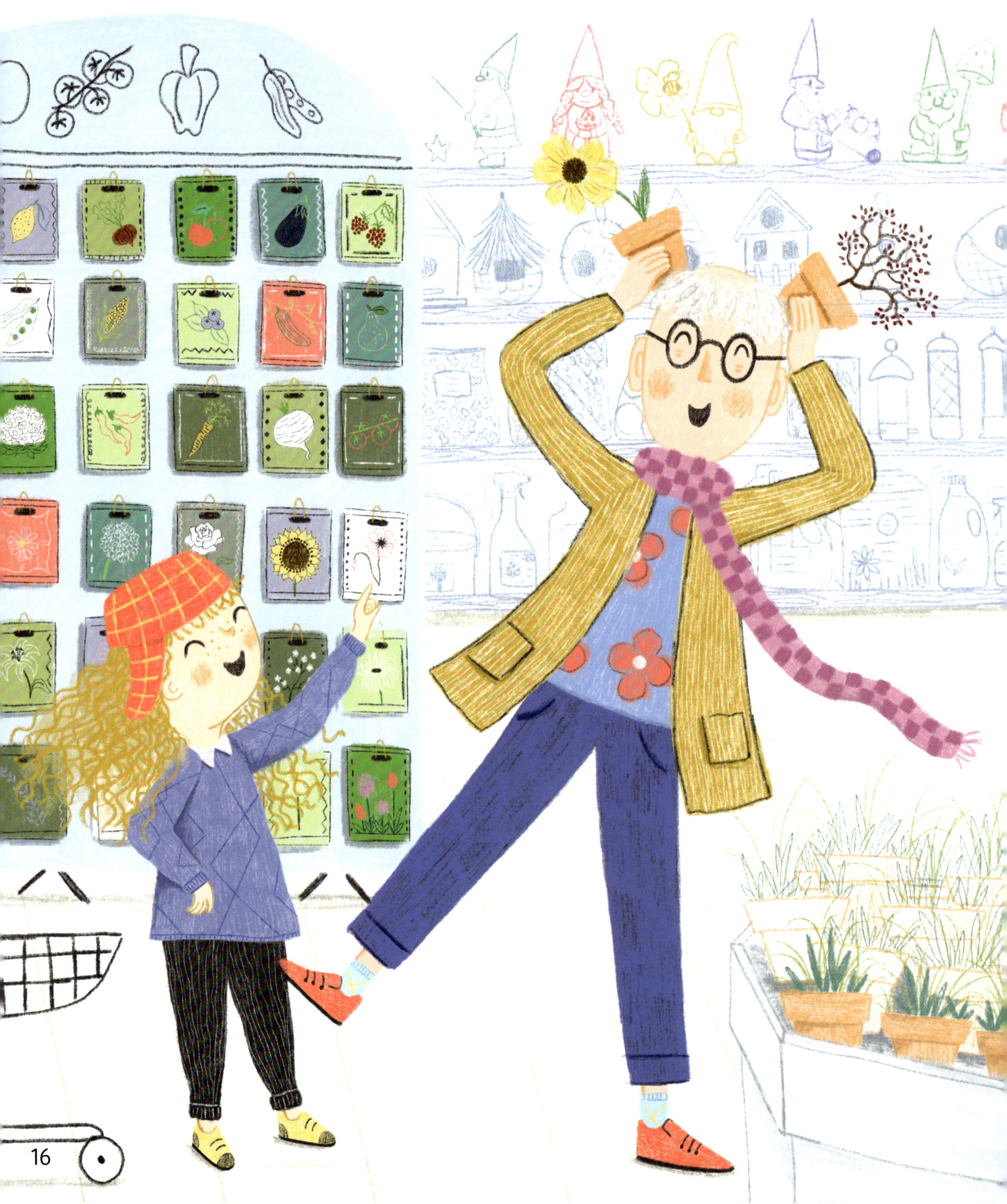

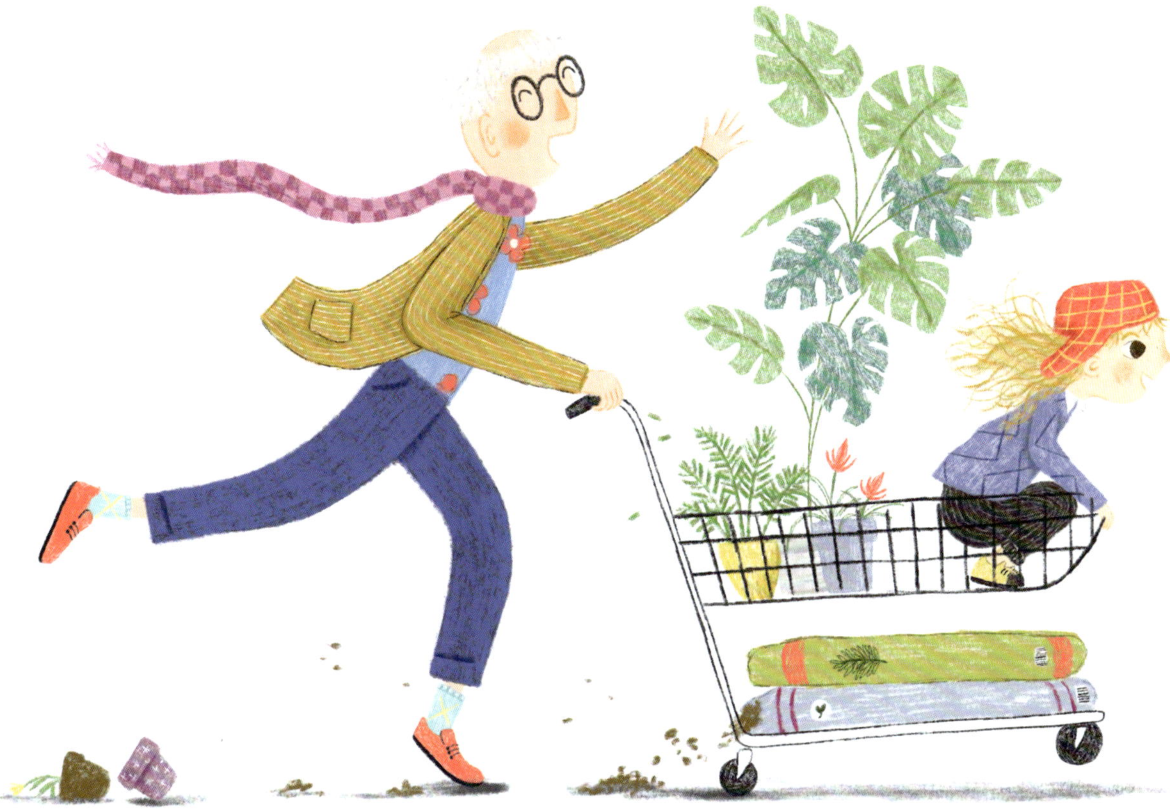

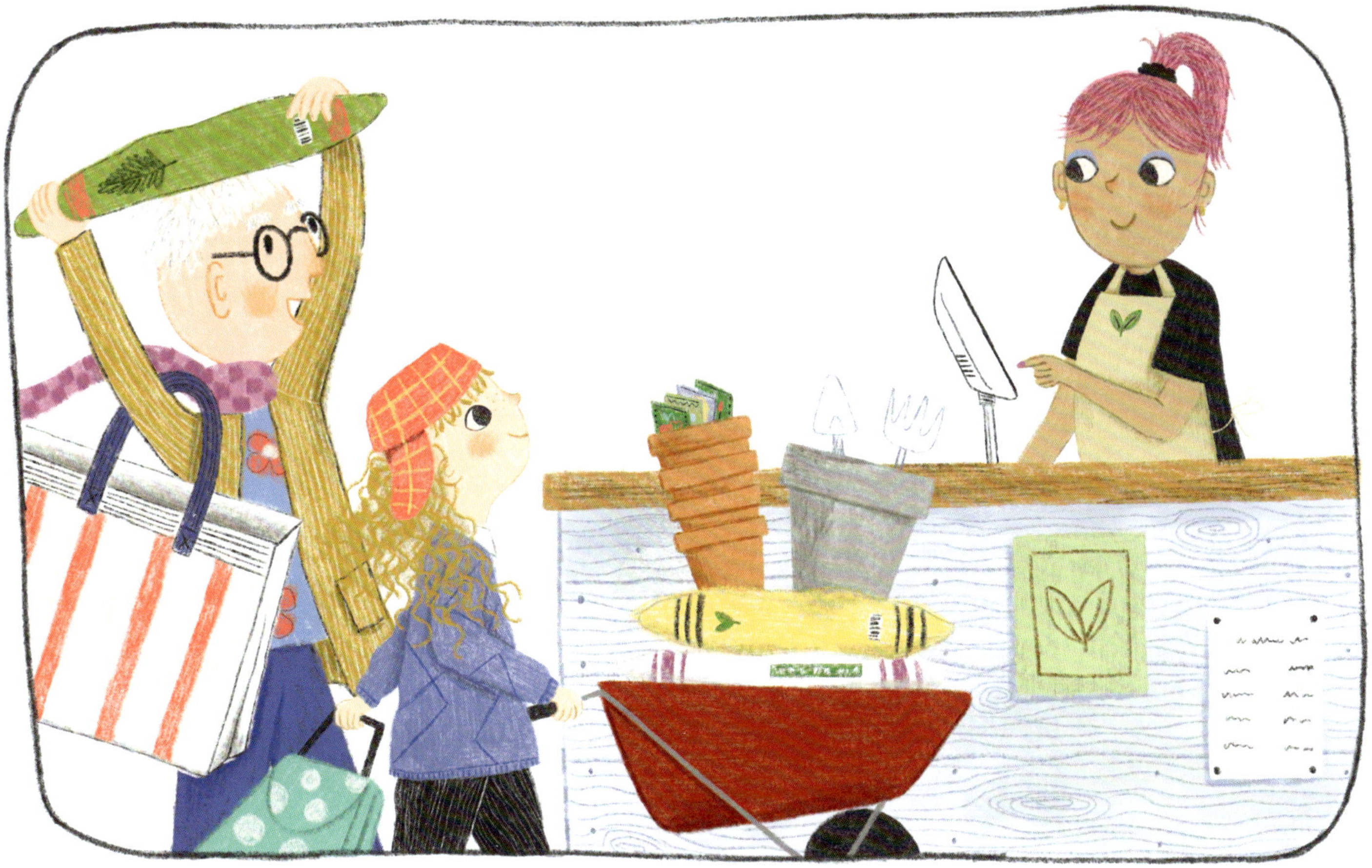

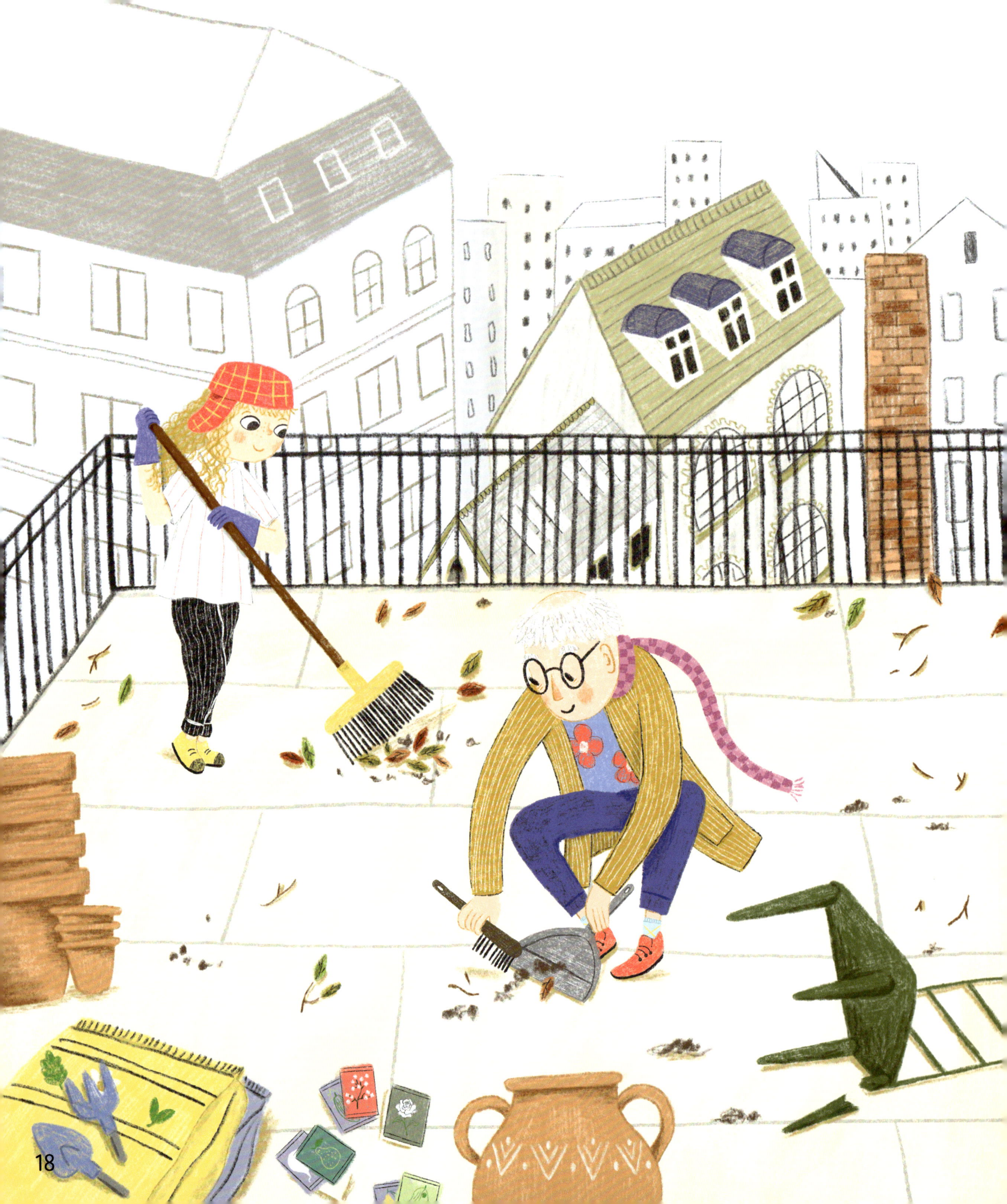

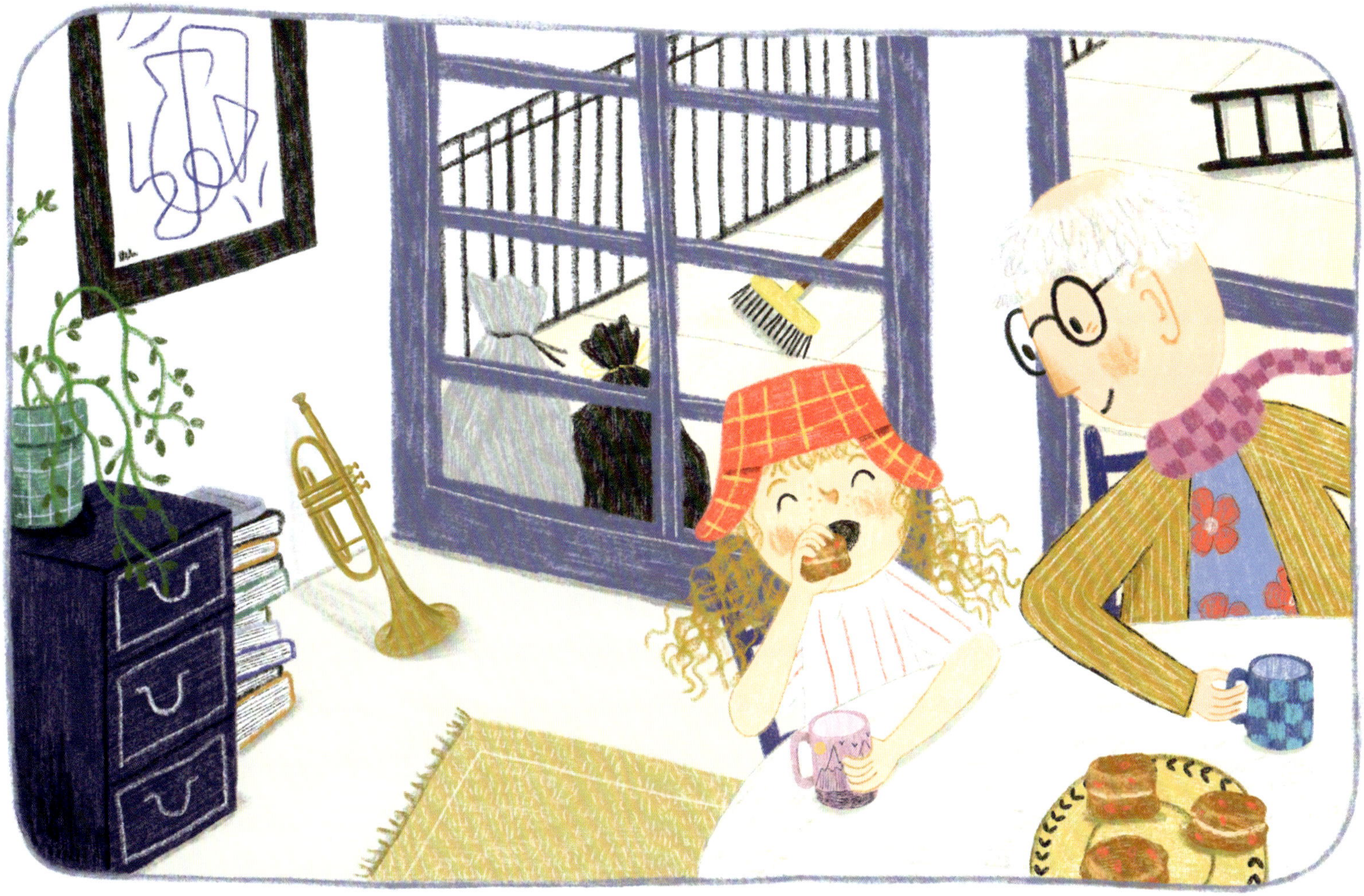

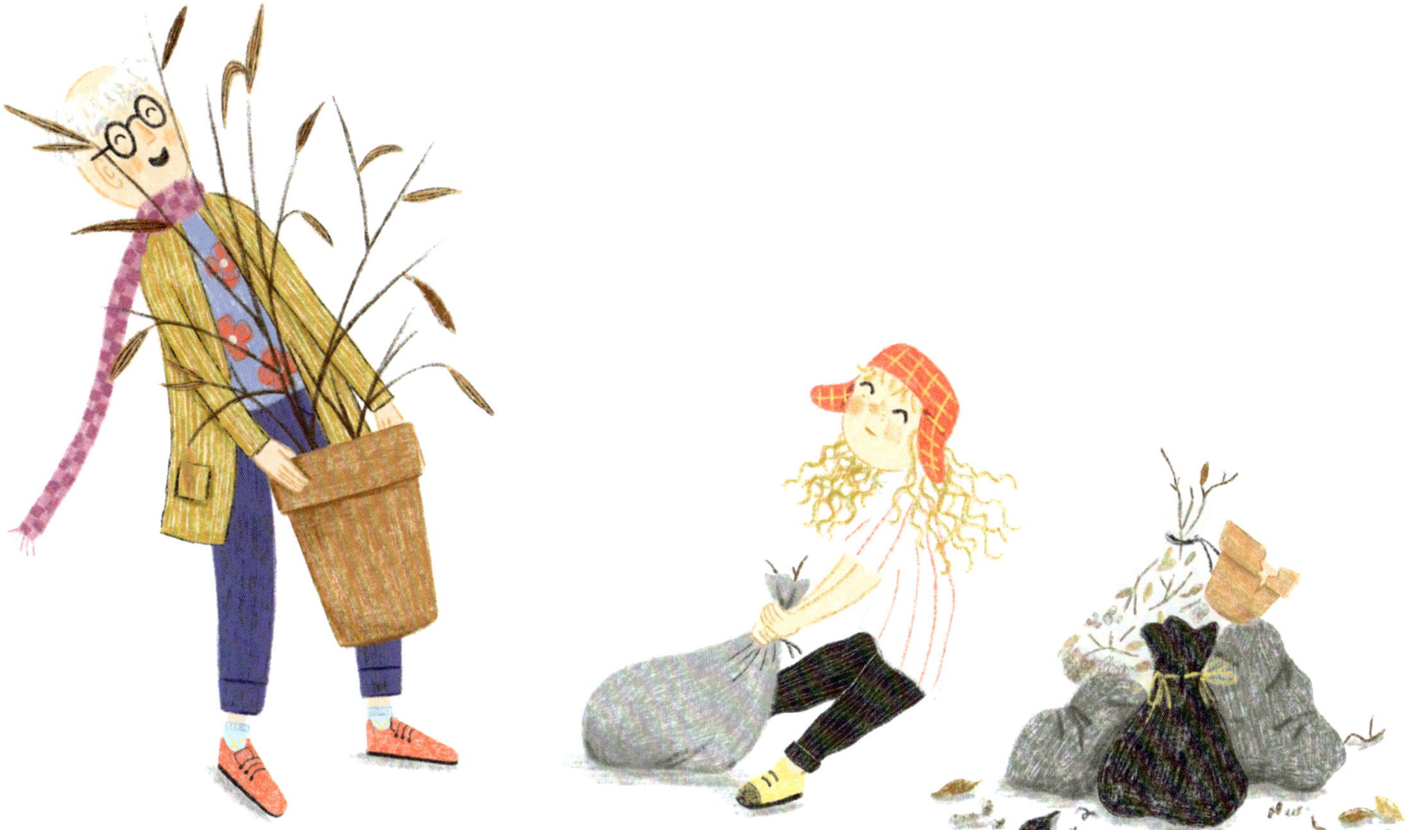

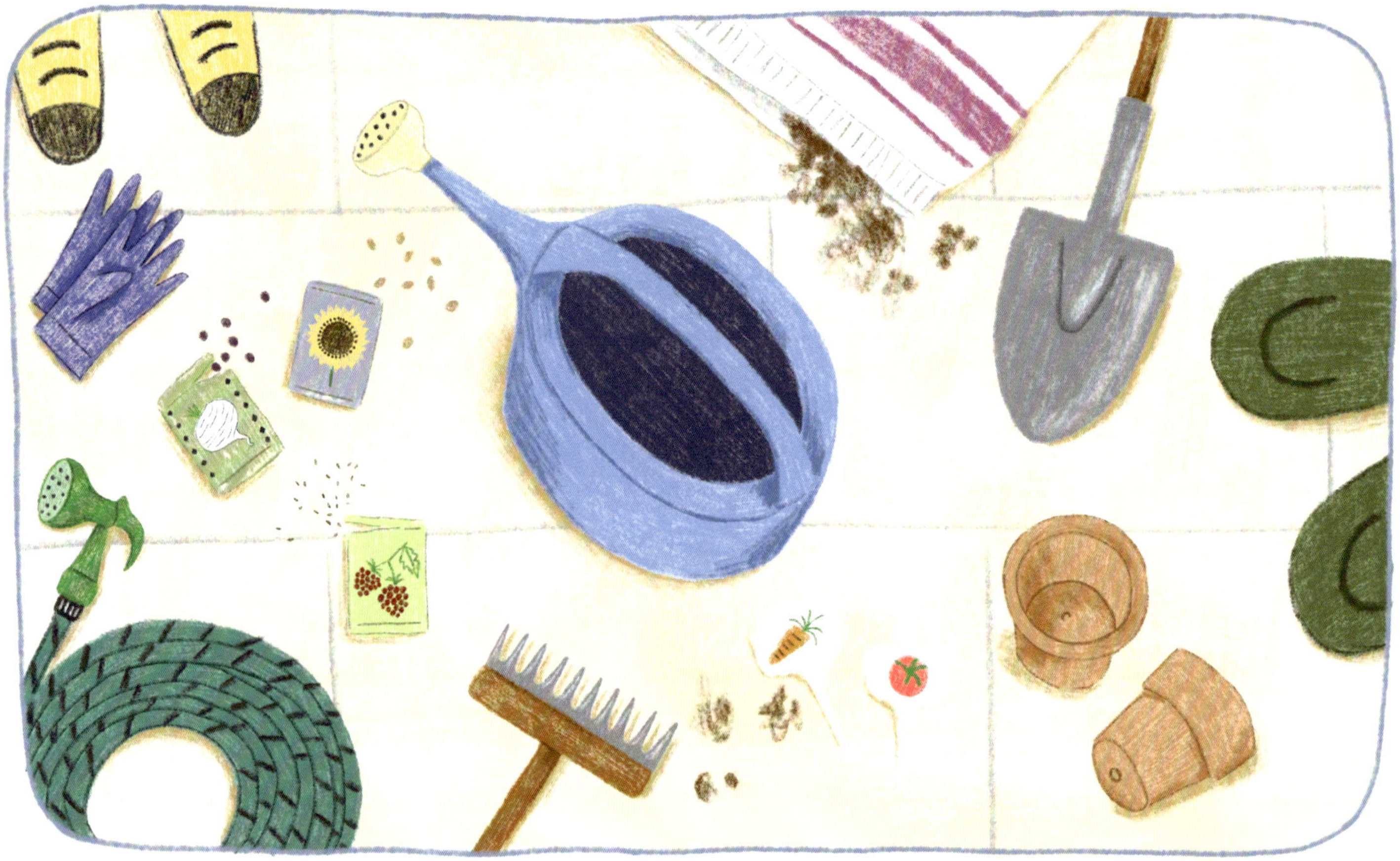

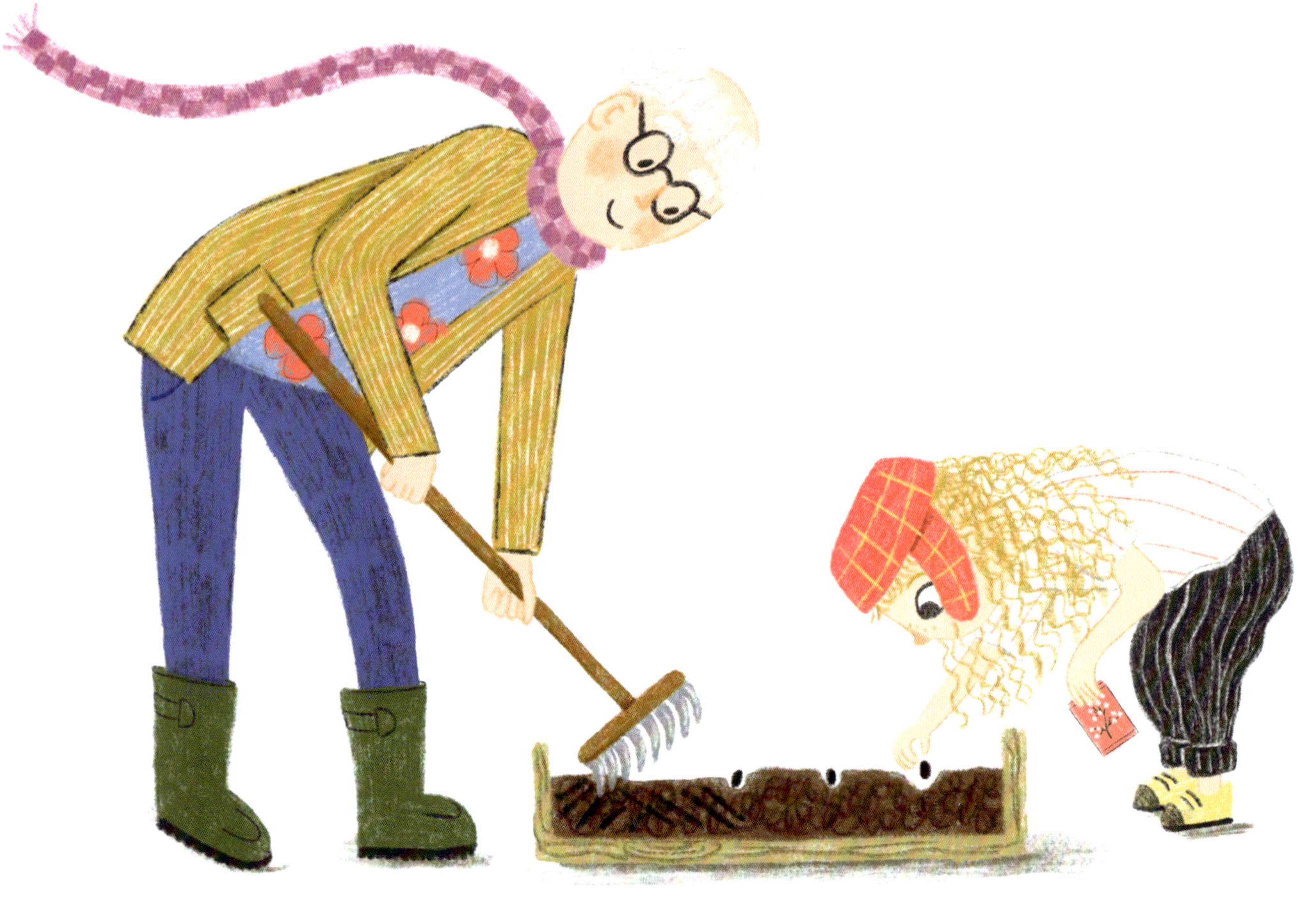

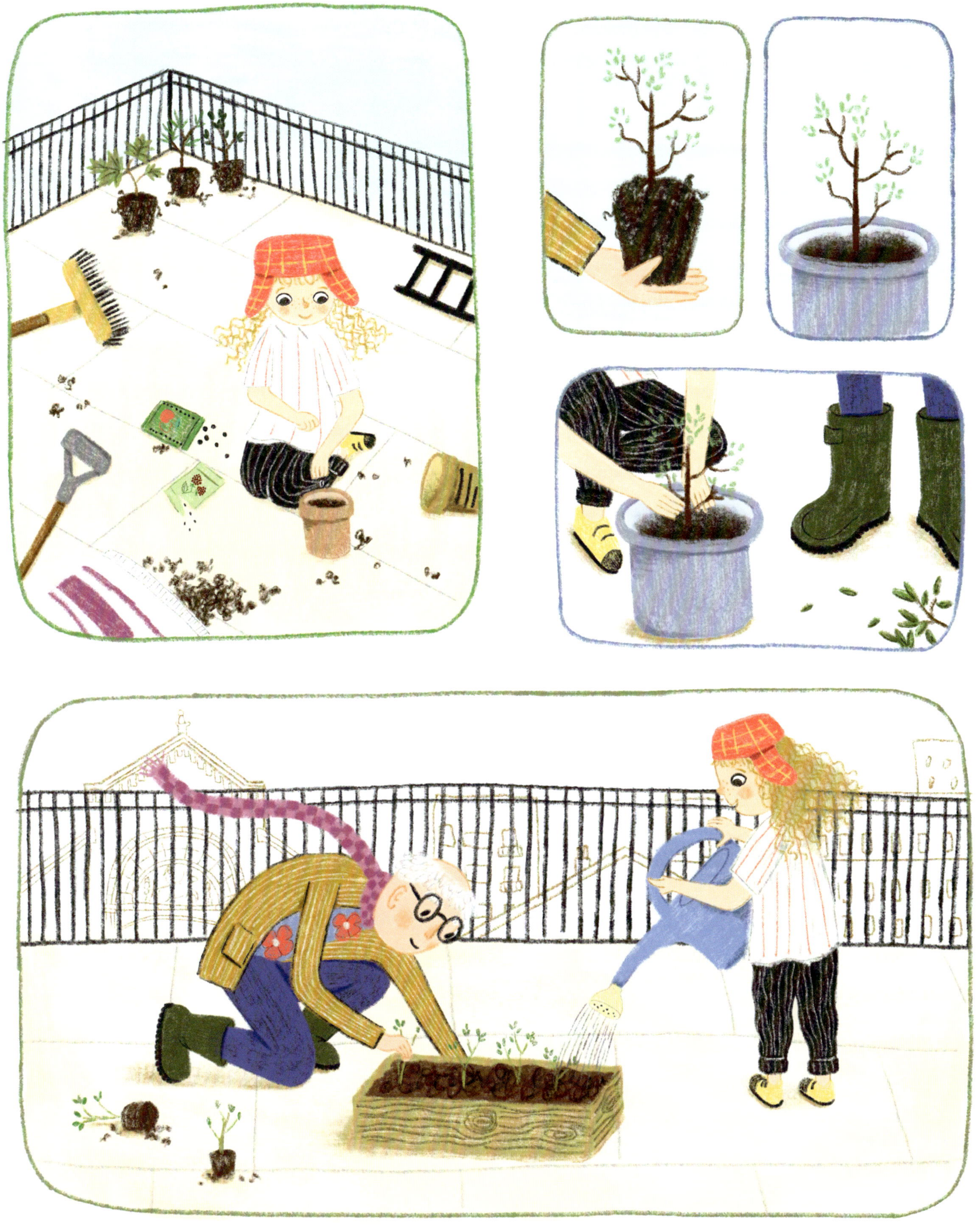

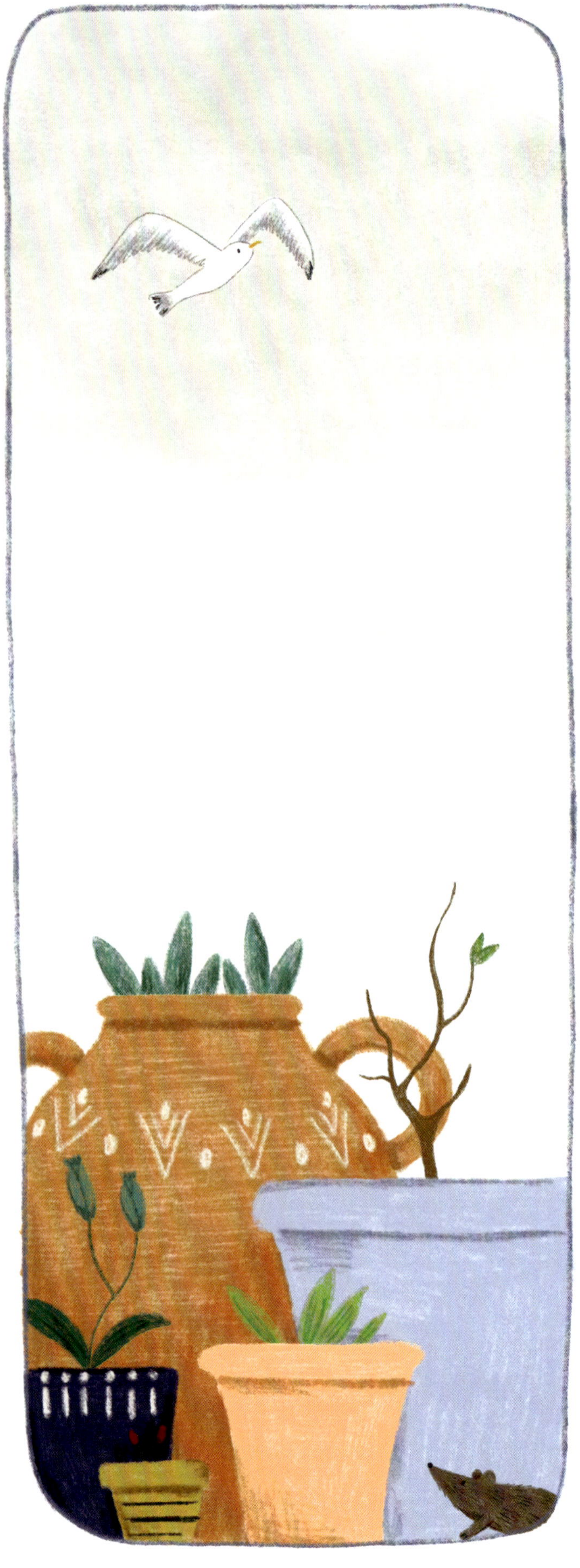

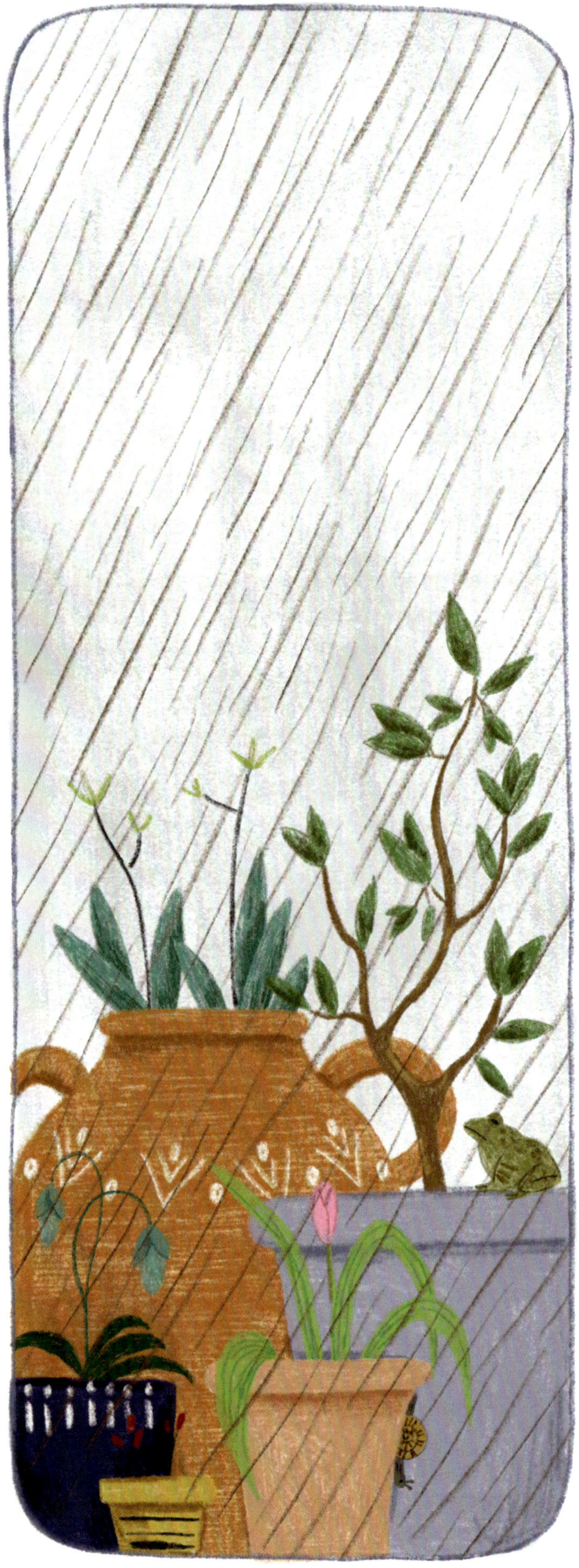

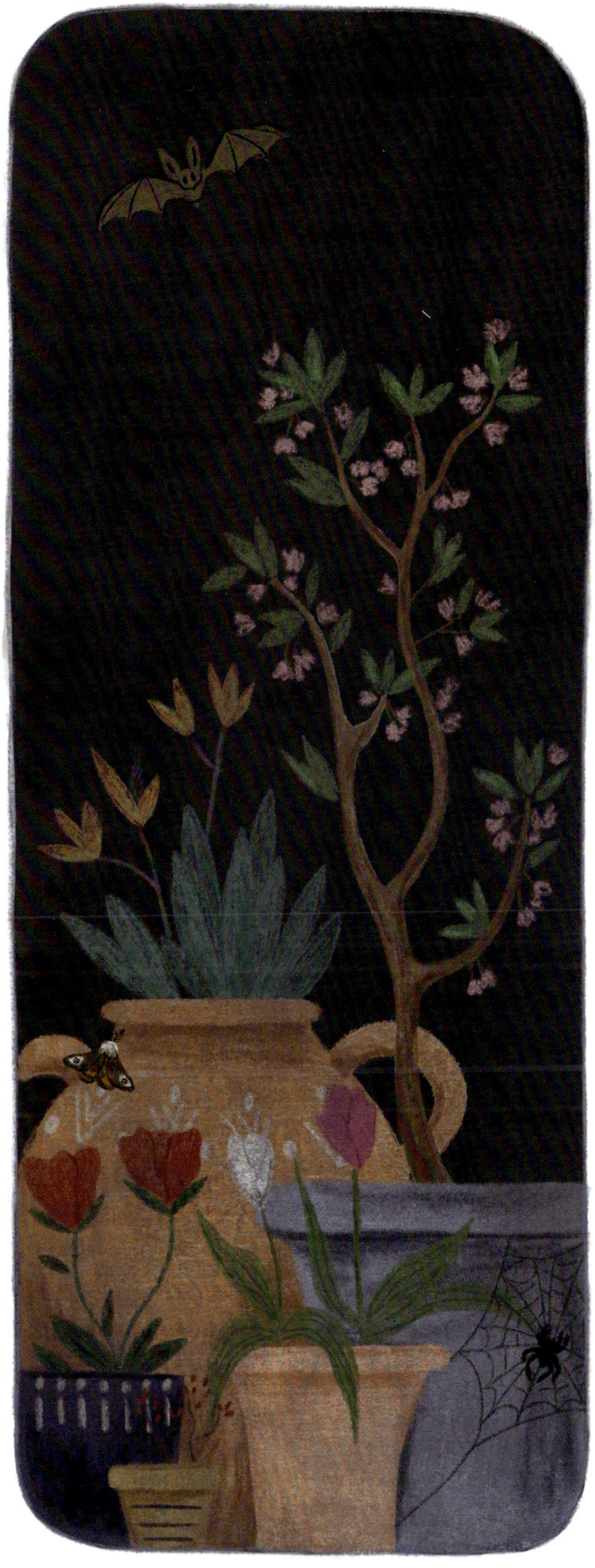

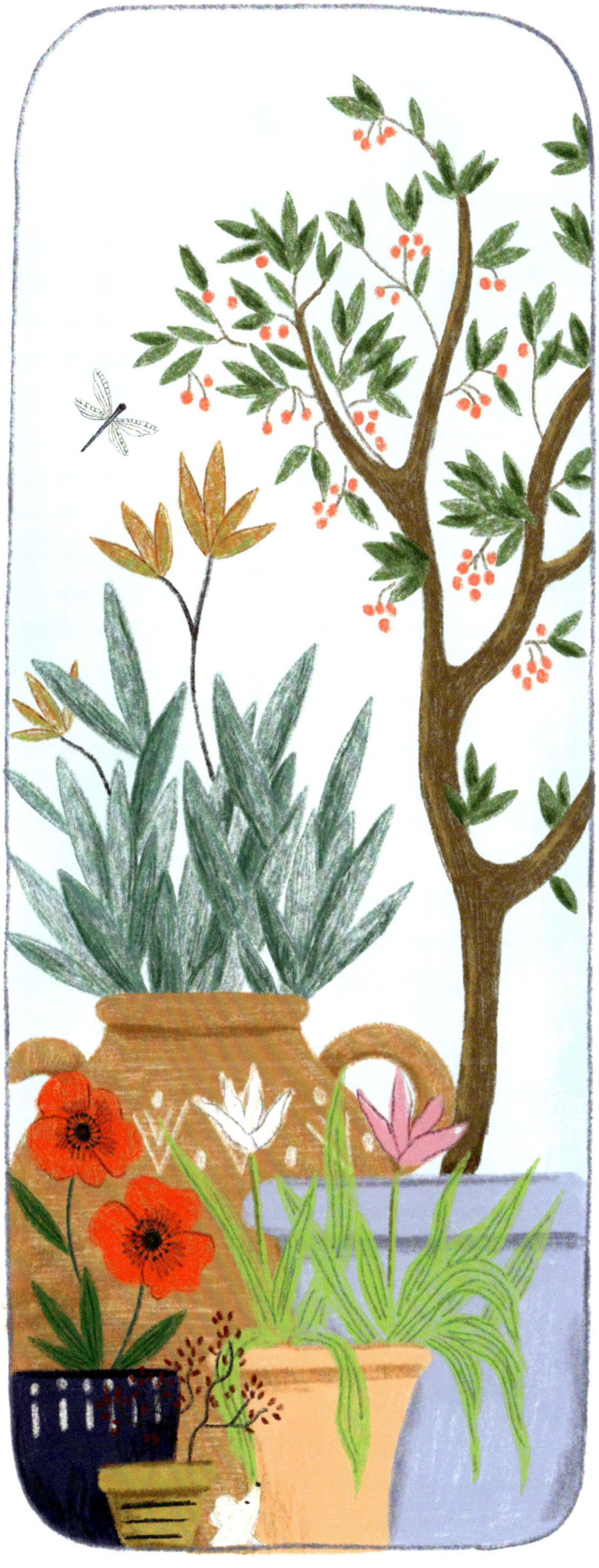

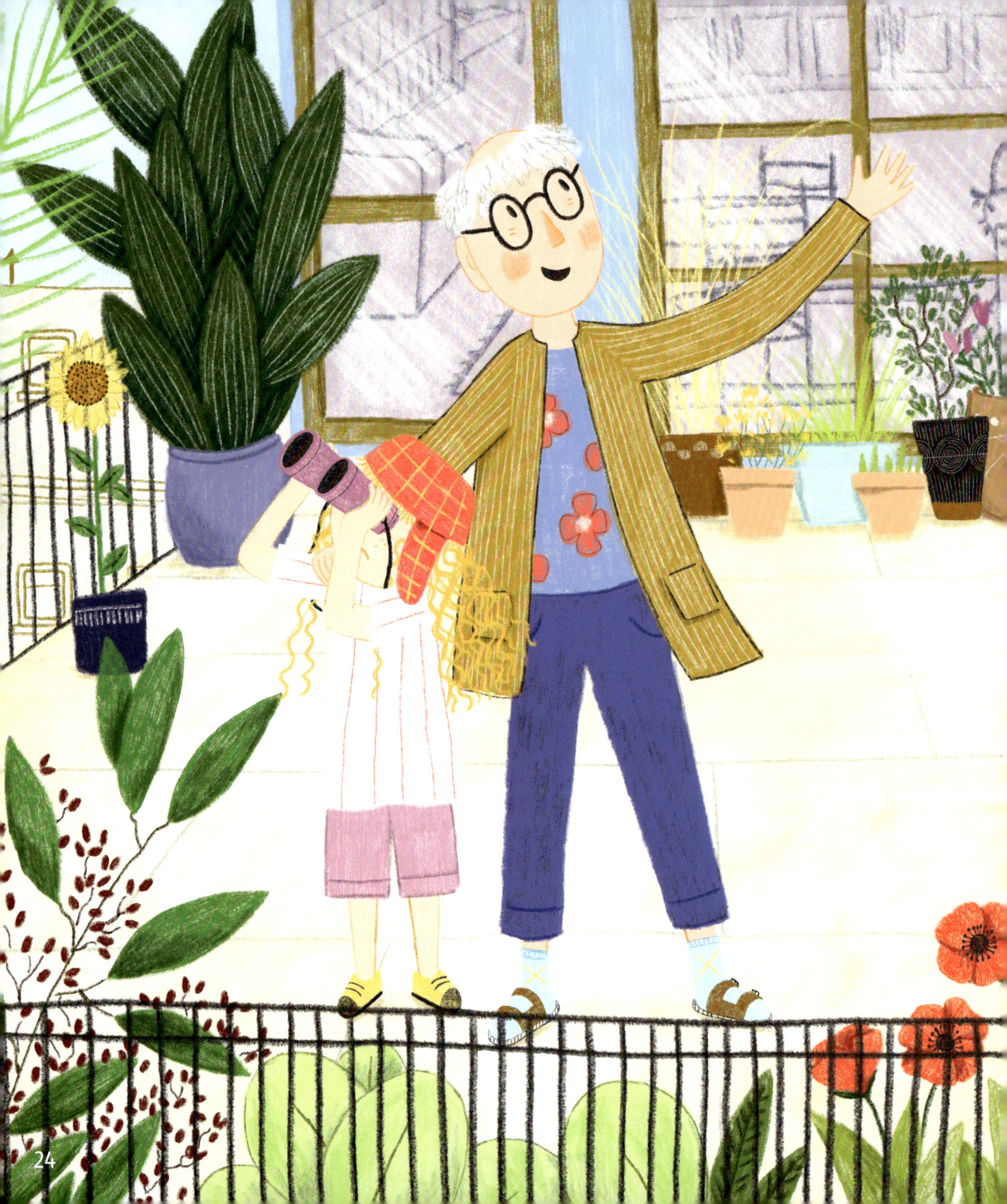

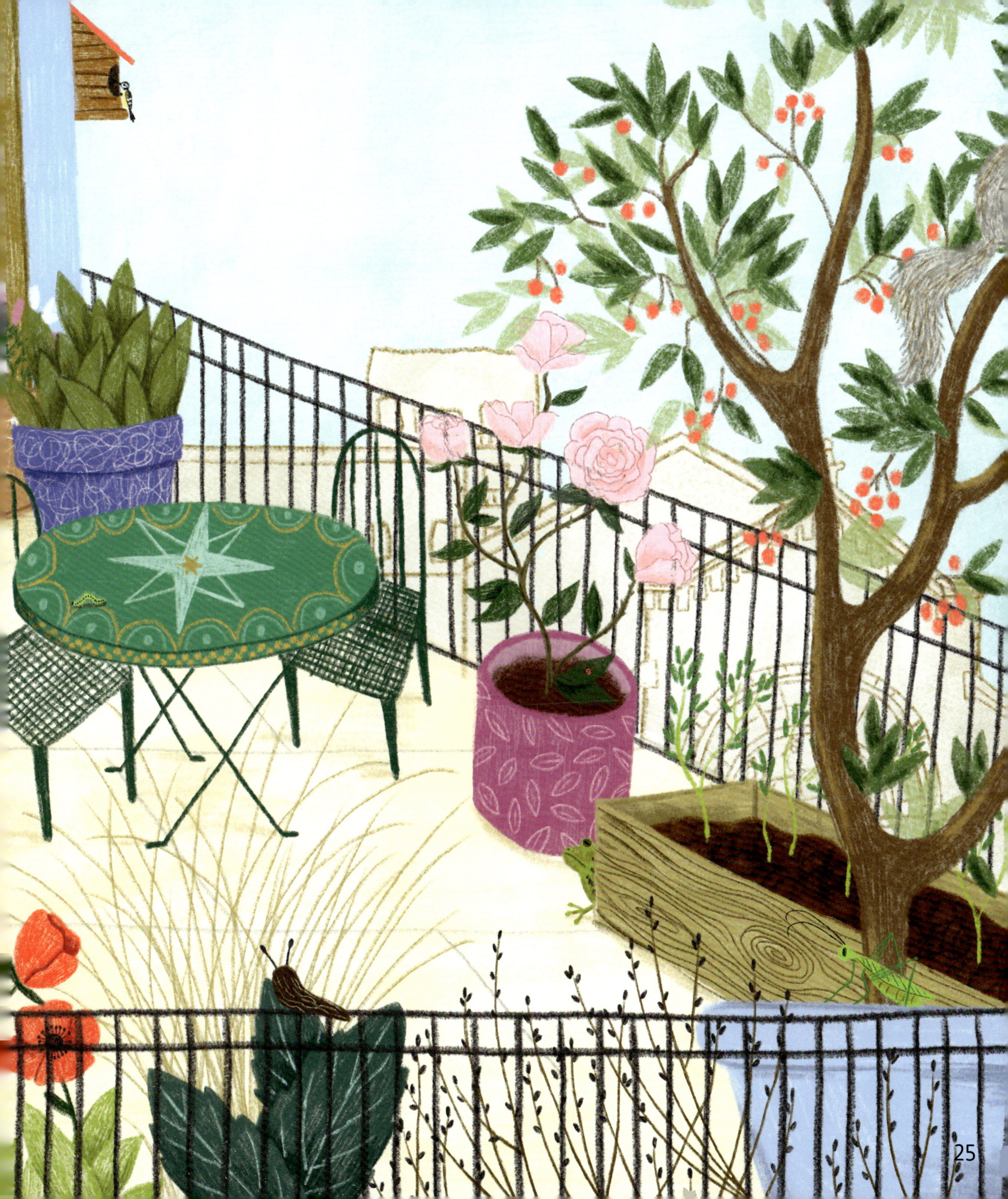

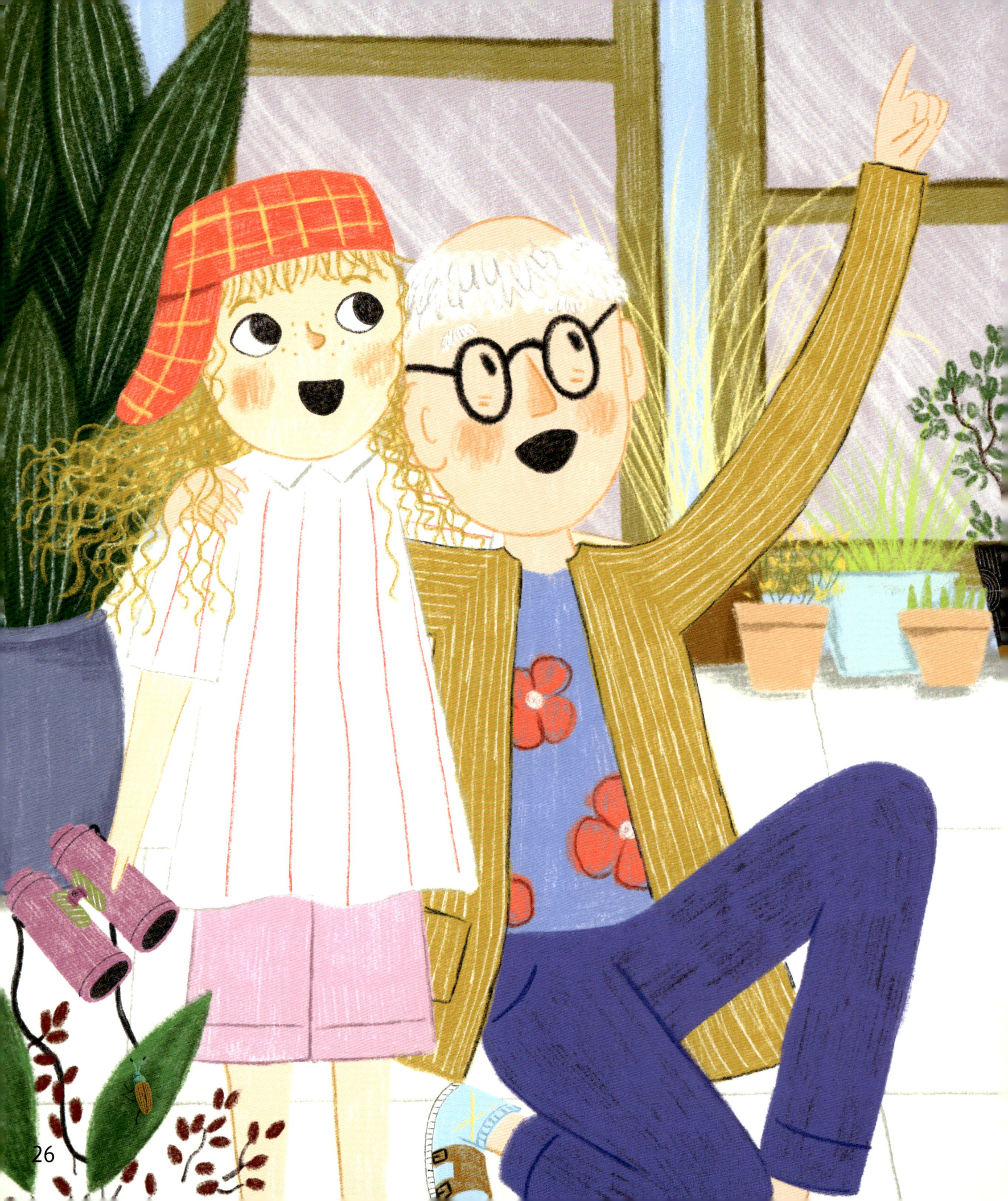

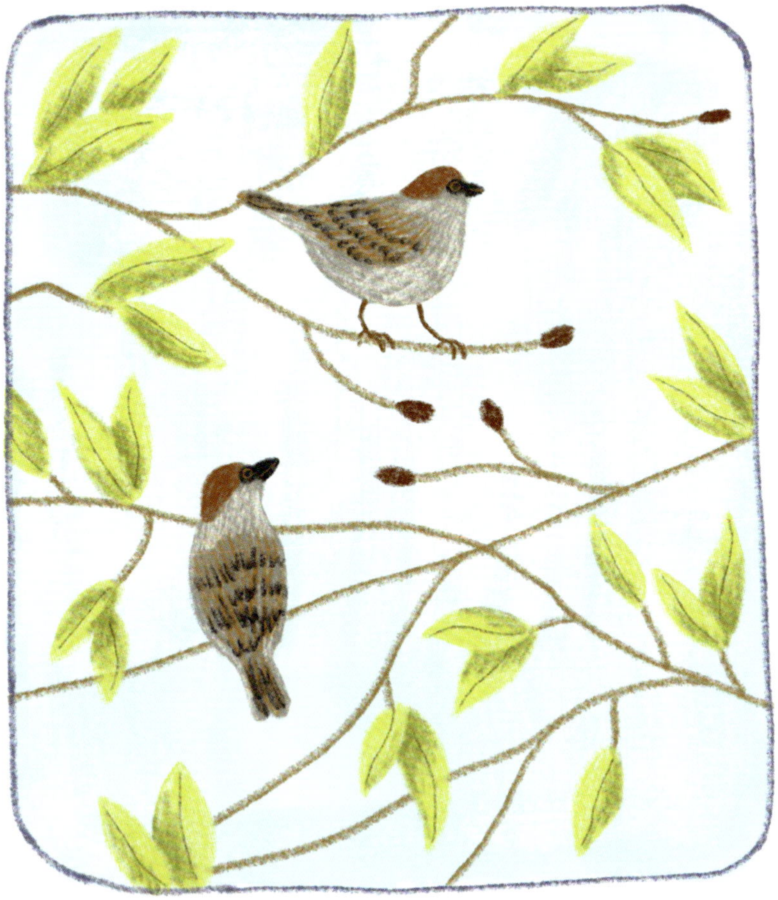
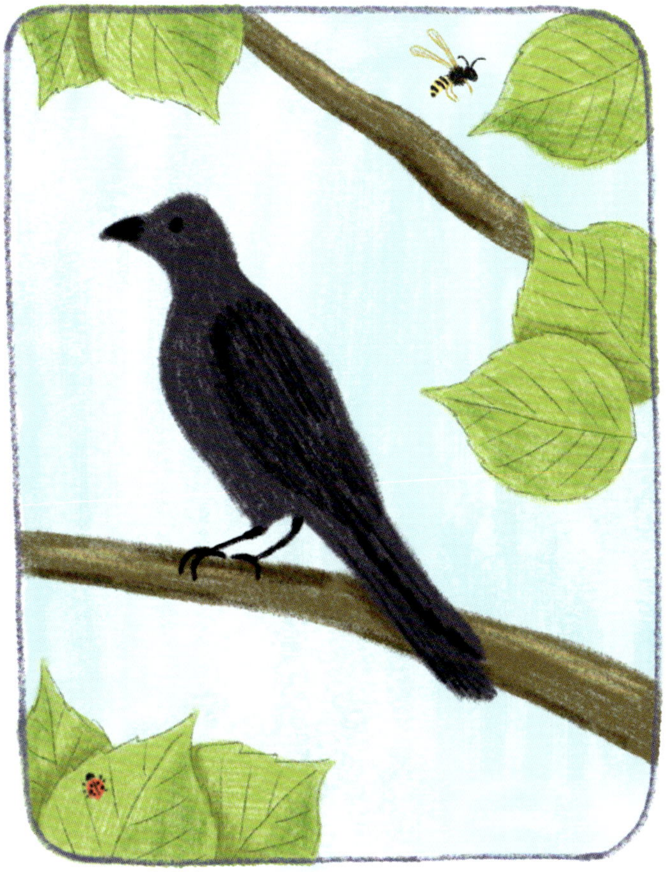
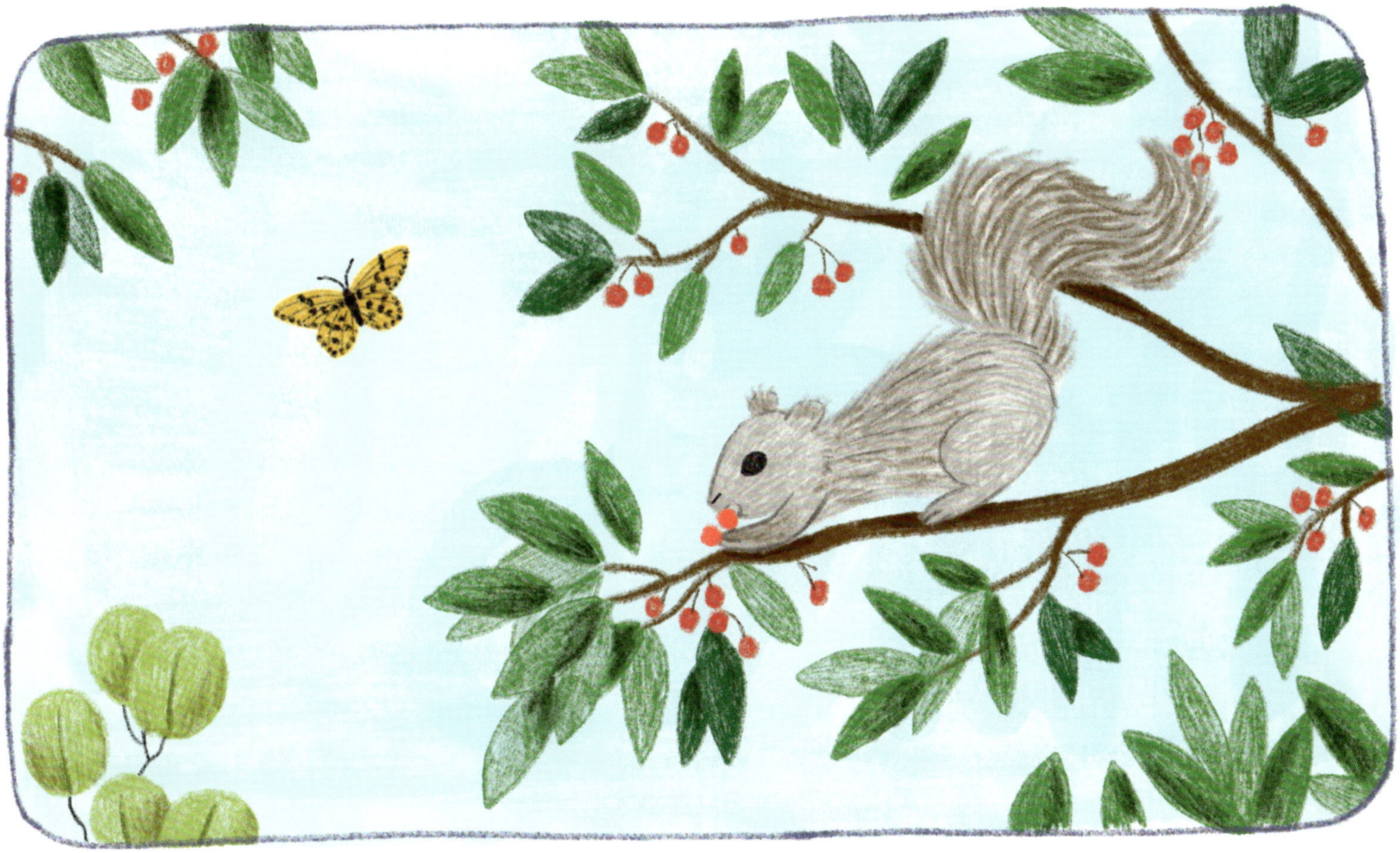

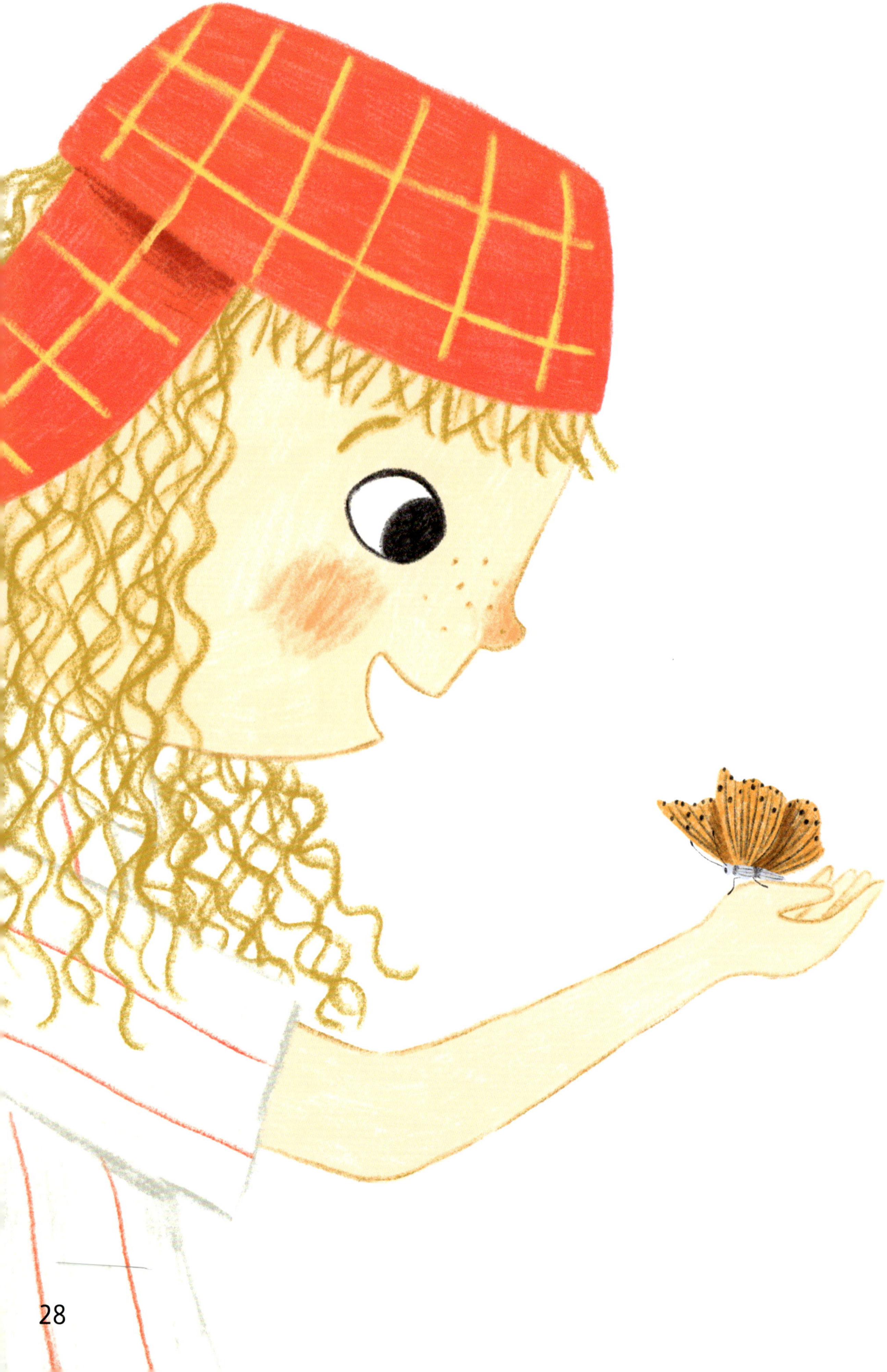

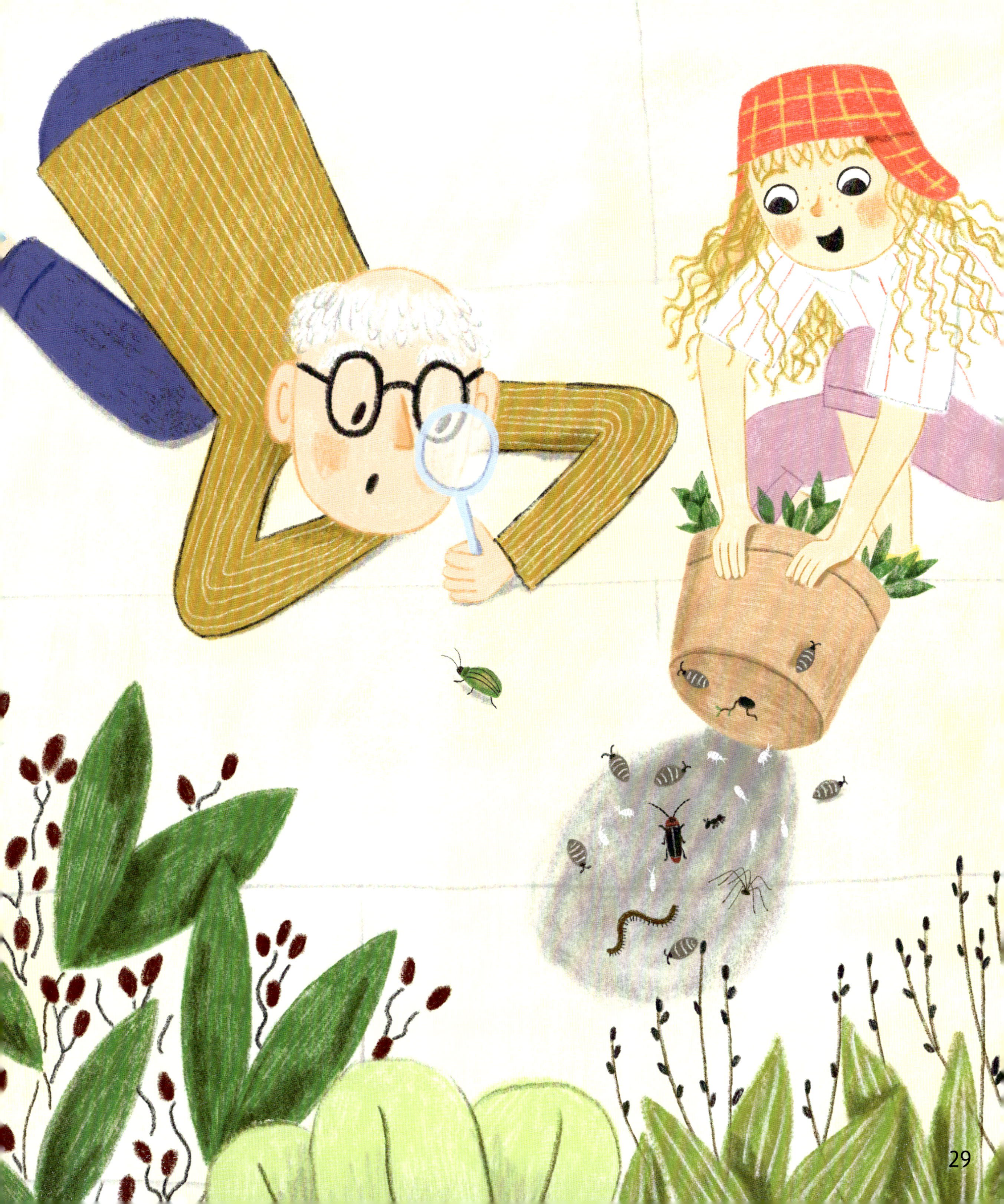

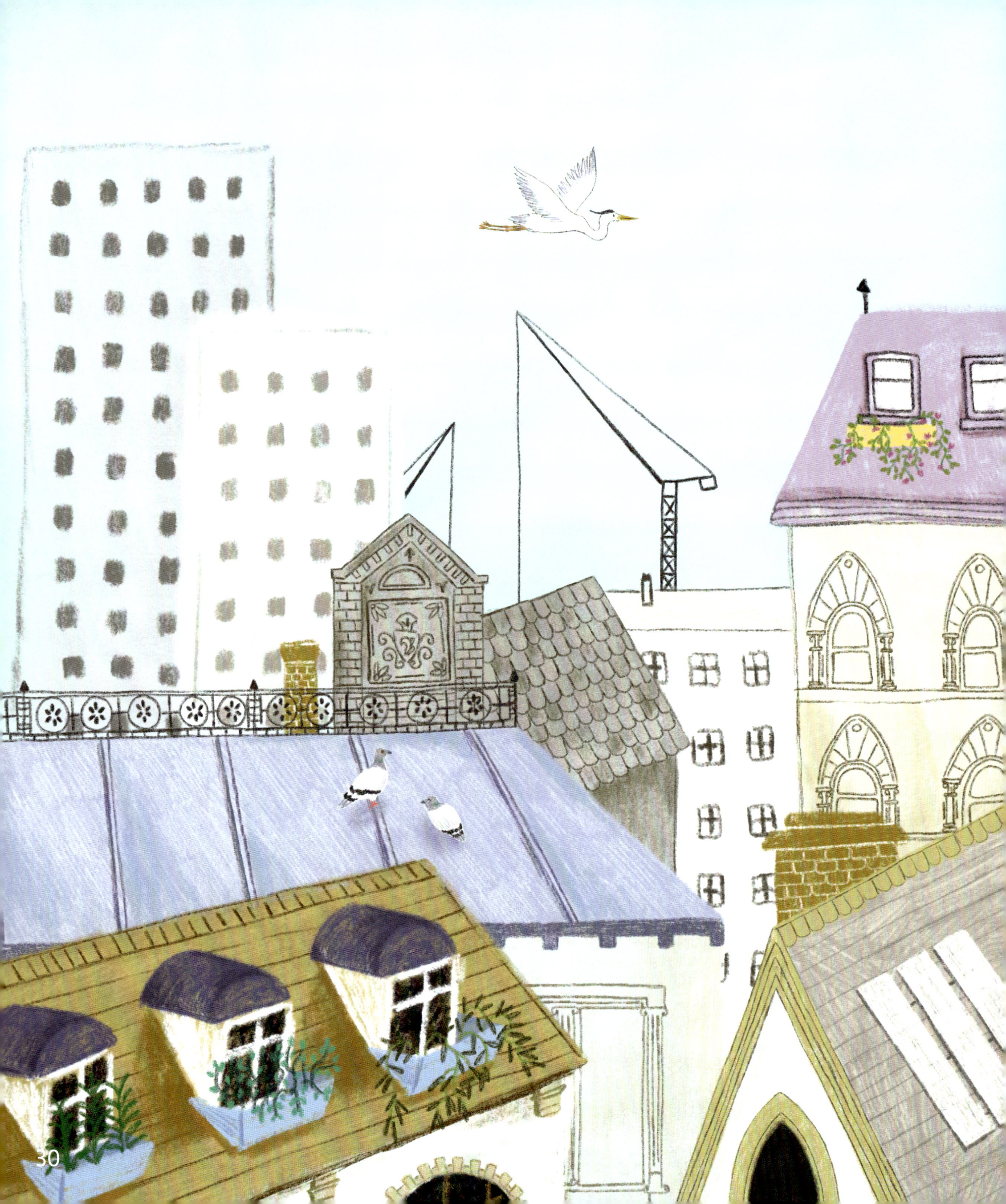

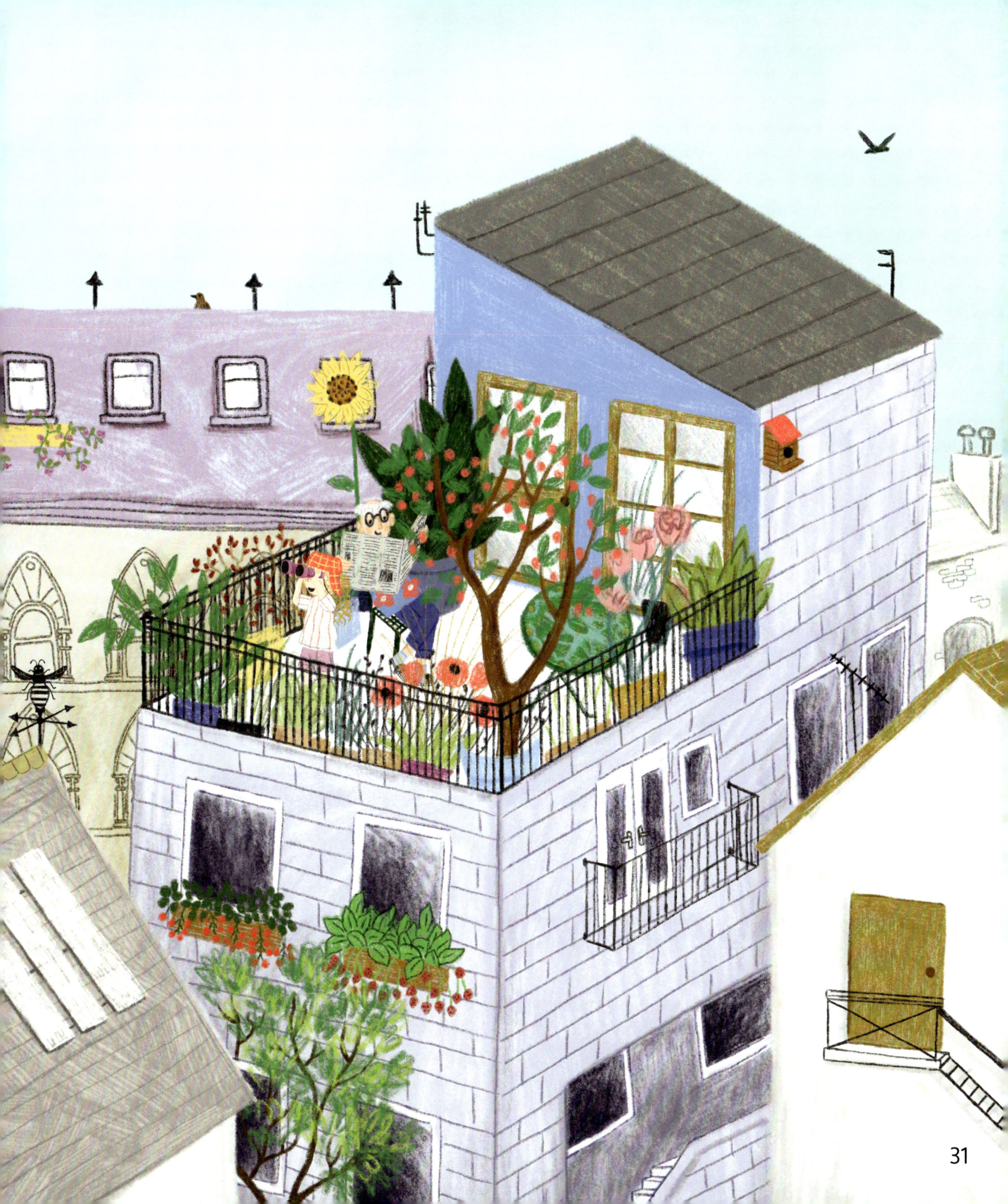

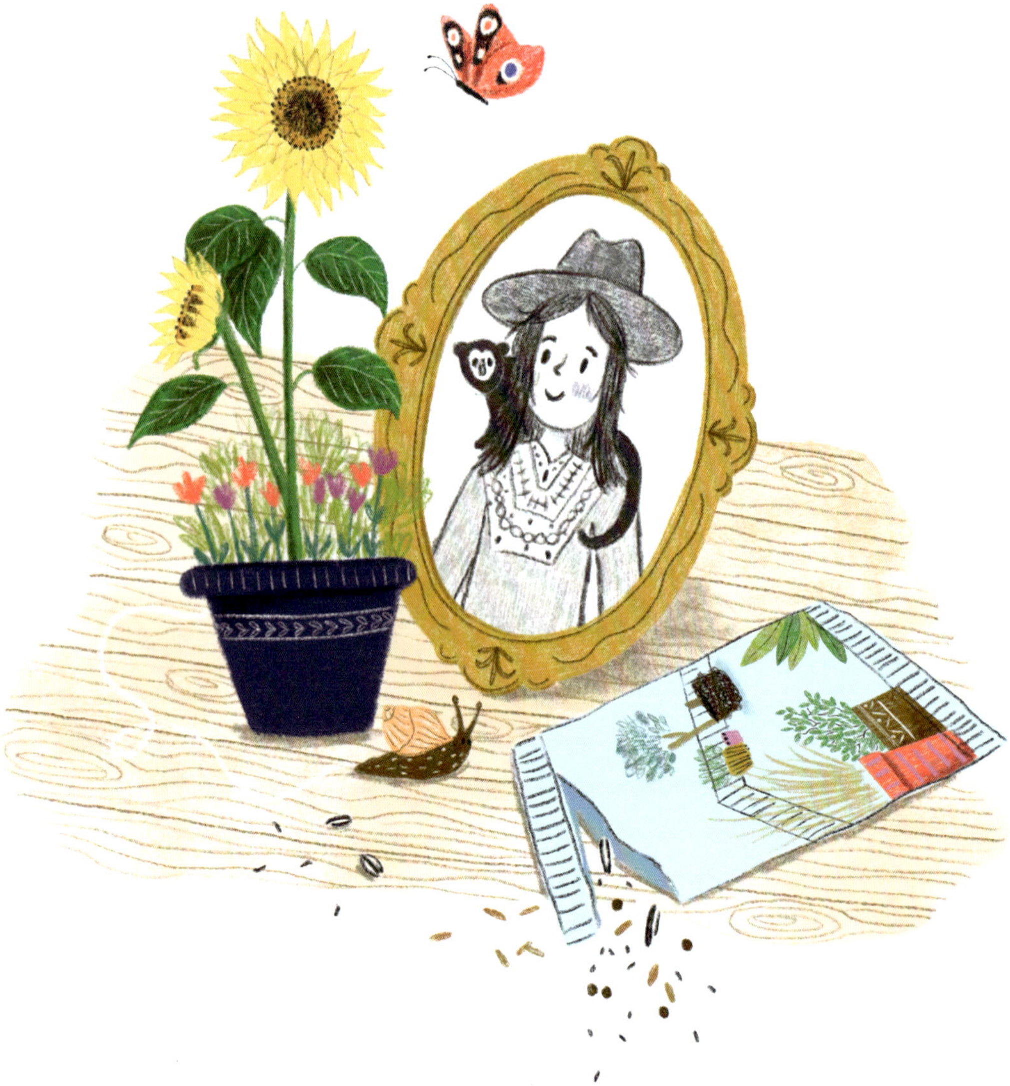